QUAN YIN
SPEAKS

QUAN YIN SPEAKS

Are You Ready?

Shih Yin

Edited by Edith Billups
Cover art by Gaelyn Larrick

Library of Congress Control Number:		2014904691
ISBN:	Hardcover	978-1-4931-8512-2
	Softcover	978-1-4931-8513-9
	eBook	978-1-4931-8511-5

This book was printed in the United States of America.

Rev. date: 03/11/2014

To order additional copies of this book, contact:
Xlibris LLC
1-888-795-4274
www.Xlibris.com
Orders@Xlibris.com
552253

CONTENTS

Acknowledgements..9
Introduction...11

PART ONE
Setting the Stage

Chapter One: Why? 23
Chapter Two: The Soul's Earth Adventures...........................36
Chapter Three: Reincarnation, the Karmic Wheel and
    The Akashic Hall of Records 44
Chapter Four: The Journey of the Warrior 52

PART TWO
The Great Shift

Chapter one: The Eleventh Hour 63
Chapter Two: The Lotus Connection 73
Chapter Three: The Challenge of Chaos...............................83
Chapter Four: The Enigma of 2012 91

PART THREE
The Ladder of Evolution

Chapter One: Perception...99
Chapter Two: The Ego Mantra..103
Chapter Three: Rewiring the Panel.................................109
Chapter Four: The Merkabah Vehicle..............................123
Chapter Five: The Communication Network 130

PART FOUR
The Construction Platform

Chapter One: Transition 141
Chapter Two: The Chrysalis Rebirth 148
Chapter Three: Spaceship Earth 158
Chapter Four: Lotus Petals 164

References 179
About the Author 180

Dedication

I dedicate this book to the Goddess Quan Yin, the aspect of the Divine Feminine Creator Goddess and to Mother Mary, the embodiment of the Divine Mother. Without the encouragement and the divine, loving support of these two great divine aspects of Love and Compassion this book could not have been written.

ACKNOWLEDGEMENTS

I wish to thank the generosity of the many great masters who encouraged and supported the work of the Goddess Pathway. I thank Tyberon, the Earth Keeper for sharing the information given byMetratron. I thank Ronna Herman for the messages from Archangel Michael and Lee Carroll forthe Kryon channels. Their gifts of channelled information are much needed at this time in the human history of evolution.

I would also like to acknowledge the EHF Master Teachers who bravely continue to walk the Goddess Path with courageous commitment to their own healing journey and dedication in helping others who ask for assistance along the path.

I am deeply grateful and touched by the support of all these Masters who walk the earth during this challenging time of the Great Shift in Consciousness.

INTRODUCTION

In order to have a greater understanding of what this book is all about, I felt it necessary to share parts of my life. To condense the events I apologize beforehand for the uneven sequential time line of my short autobiography.

I consider my life to be an amazing miracle and hope that you will agree with me when you hear my story. I was born on an island off the South-Eastern coast of Sumatra in Indonesia and am of Chinese ancestry. My ancestors from both my parents were Chinese traders who sailed the ancient southern trade-routes and ended settling on one of the islands on the equator. For the first five years of my life I was brought up by my maternal grandmother. She did not follow the traditional Buddhist faith but would adapt the philosophy of the Buddha to her own intuitive way of life. She did recognize the Goddess Quan Yin as the female energy of the Buddha but did not choose to worship at any formal temples. I grew up with the memory of the altars that my grandmother and my mother created in the garden during specific Buddhist days of ancestral worship. The best memories for me as a child were, of course, the abundance of mouth-watering foods that were prepared for special ceremonial occasions.

I had to leave the tranquil island home of my grandmother when I was brought back to my parents at the age of five. Work was dwindling on the island for the younger generation and my parents moved to Jakarta, the capital city, where my father was able to find work. He had to provide for a household of nine people that included, in addition to himself, six children, my aunt and my mother. We had no home for the first few years when we moved to the city and had to live in a shack in my uncle's front yard. We were fortunate that my mother's brothers were very successful businessmen and would occasionally extend a helping hand to their sister. She had five brothers who could help, and it used to frustrate and irritate them to watch their sister trying to take care of a struggling household. There was not always an abundance of food for all the growing children and the occasional leftovers that were sent our way were eagerly greeted in anticipation of having a full belly that day. As I mentioned earlier, the special foods prepared on the days of worship to the Buddha and the ancestors were times of celebration indeed.

My parents were both well-educated and understood the importance of education for their children, at any cost. The only option for a good education was through private schools run by various missionary churches. My cousins were already attending these private schools and again, my uncles came to the rescue. First I was sent to a Dutch Protestant School, then to a Catholic Convent School. Next came an English school taught by Hindu teachers and finally it was back to the convent to complete my education.

We lived in a Muslim country and many of my friends were of the Islamic faith. It was not until much later in life that I realized how fortunate I was to have been exposed to all the prominent world religions providing me with an extraordinary outlook on life.

After the Second World War, the political situation in the country was deteriorating rapidly and those of us of Chinese heritage became fearful as violence erupted against the Chinese communities. The rich Chinese families immediately sent their children out of the country to the Western world, mainly to the USA and Europe. For the poor, it was devastating and a time of great anxiety as they caught a glimpse of a frightening future.

As a young adult, I was one among those who had to face and walk through the experience of the dark times. For a long time, I felt utter hopelessness. Despair descended upon me after experiencing discrimination, being placed under house arrest, and undergoing interrogations that lasted for days. I knew that I could not survive this storm of prejudice, persecution and violent hostility that raged all around me. Yet at times, amidst all the turmoil, there were periods of hope that were like pinpricks of light against a black screen. During those rare moments I was able to find a sense of quiet wait-fullness as if I was able to put myself into the eye of the storm. I did not understand, and did not realize how protected I was, as I walked through this valley of dark shadows.

In school I was introduced to the Christian Bible, to God, Jesus and Mary. I embraced and immersed myself into this new faith. My prayers kept me in a sanctuary of peace and my strong faith was a protective armor that cloaked me against the violence. Somehow deep inside me, I knew that I would escape this dark pool of human misery and suffering. I remembered that my grandmother and my aunt, who lived with her, used to pray to the Goddess Quan Yin. Being newly initiated into what I considered a better path, however my prayers were mainly directed to Mary, the Holy Mother. During those challenging days I accepted without question the fact that I could sense her presence, and I thought that every church member could as well. I looked upon her as the ideal loving Mother and dreamt about and bared my soul to her in my prayers.

Then one day the first stages of my miracle began to unfold. I found myself standing on the deck of a cruise ship waving good-bye to my parents, aunts and cousins. I was sailing away on a Northwest voyage, leaving everyone and everything that I had ever known in my life with the awareness that I might never return. I had a one way ticket bought by my father with the bonus money he had earned because of his ability to read and write in English. I carried one suitcase filled with some strange hand-me-down clothing, items called "panty hose", "woolen sweaters" and a winter coat. I had no clue how to use them and no idea what my life would be like in this country called Germany that was to be my new home. My prayers from that day onward were of deep gratitude and thanksgiving, for to me a miracle did enter my life.

I spend the next two years in Germany and marvelled at the generosity and friendliness of the people I met. They opened their doors and welcomed me into their homes. I learned to appreciate their food and accepted their loving friendship. I learned all about their culture and their customs and found that they believed in many of the same things I believed in. For the first time in my life, I woke up feeling safe, and I was even given special sweet treats to enjoy that I didn't have to fight for. However, somehow I never felt at home in this country and sensed that there was something else waiting for me. I dutifully attended Mass and all the rituals of the Catholic faith and continued my prayers to the Virgin Mother. I firmly believed that the miracle in my life happened through her intervention, and I was forever grateful to her.

Two years later, I found myself searching again for a new place to live. My two year contract had expired, and there was no renewal possible. I did not have enough money and could not meet the required entry fee for immigration demanded by many other countries. I had to find a new home fast. Then, lo and behold, another miracle happened, and although on a much smaller scale I considered it as still part of my miracle. Canada had suddenly changed its immigration policy, and my siblings and I could now enter and call this great Northern Country our final destination. I finally felt as if I had reached my true home. I was astonished to find out that the government of my new country was giving me money to go to school and complete my education. I had to pay it back upon graduation, of course, but it was an interest free loan. I considered myself fortunate and blessed that another big part of my miracle had manifested in my life.

It seemed as if the miracles continued to appear as I began my new life. I graduated and immediately was offered a great job as a primary school teacher in a Catholic school. A few years later I met and married a wonderful partner who loved me. I did not think that anyone could, or would love me, for I did not consider myself an attractive female. My Ego-self-esteem then was still on the low scale of awareness.

Years passed, and my life was full. I lived the life of a suburban, North American working housewife, and it seemed as if all my dreams had come to fruition. Then the dream bubble burst one day.

It came as a thief in the night, these dark smoky tendrils of feelings of unhappy restlessness that suddenly seeped and snuck into my thought patterns. It was feelings of something uncompleted, a sense that I was missing something I should have paid attention to. Something was wrong with me; I was not complete and I did not know what it was, or why. These discordant notes escalated and exploded into a classical spiritual awakening process through a major illness. Family and friends rallied around me, and I began to sense the gentle touch of the Goddess I did not know I knew. I rejected her presence at first, giving the excuse that I was not worthy of the attention of such a Divine Holy presence. Psychic friends confirmed that she was Quan Yin, the Divine feminine aspect of the Buddha and that she had chosen me to help her. They began to channel messages for me and urged me to listen to her call. The biggest, strongest and most profound message was that I was loved and that there was no such word as unworthiness in the vocabulary of the Divine Creator God. I also found out that my life, thus far had been a period of training as I was being groomed to fulfill a contract I had agreed upon.

Finally, there was no more hesitation on my part as I acknowledged her presence in my life and accepted the role she had patiently kept for me. As I opened myself to full communication with her, my heart broke free from the bondage of lassitude and ignorance. For days I cried out with a torrent of tears, as I heard her voice and began to gain understanding of what a human life is all about. She encouraged me to study with other living Masters to acquire more confidence and to acquire the necessary required credentials that were and are still valued within human society. Her consequent messages and teachings have been profound and have given me much clarity regarding the journey we are all on and what my role is as a human messenger, healing facilitator, a teacher and a human guide.

The following pages are an introduction to the Goddess Quan Yin. It is hoped that it might provide more clarity as to who she was, is, what she stands for, and why she has come to the fore front in this era of great change.

The Lore, the Legend and the Story of the Goddess Quan Yin

As in many legends, there are many versions of the story, for the truth lies shrouded in the mists of time. The lore, told and retold countless times, has travelled through many minds and was influenced by many diverse cultures and customs of men. The following story is one that resonates with me, and I hope that it will speak to you, as well.

As it was told, there once lived a princess in the palace of the Chinese King in ancient China. Her name was Miao-Shan. Unusual signs at her birth such as flowers falling from the sky accompanied by a delicate scent were deemed signs that a sacred incarnation was taking place. The Princess believed and embraced the teachings of the Buddha at an early age and practiced compassion and love to everyone she met including animals. The monks proclaimed her to be the reincarnation of the male form of an ancient bodhisattva known as Avalokiteshvara who came to help humanity in their suffering. According to legend, he was born with a lotus in his hand and spoke the mantra "Om Mani Padme Hum" meaning Om, the jewel in the lotus. This mantra is now the signature prayer to Quan Yin, and the lotus is considered to be her personal emblem. By the 9th century AD, the name Avalokiteshvara was translated into Kuan-Shih-Yin and later shortened to Kuan Yin, as more and more women in China began to worship the Deity who was compassionate to their plight.

Per tradition, upon the princess' eligibility to marry, the King arranged a traditional marriage for his daughter. She refused, begging him to allow her to continue with her work of mercy and compassion towards all sentient beings, animals included. The King would not budge from his decision, and the Princess Miao-Shan defied him. She took refuge in a monastery on the mountain and became a nun. Legend has it that the animals helped her in her plight.

The King was furious at his daughter's refusal to obey him. In his opinion she had betrayed him, causing him to lose his dignity and reputation as a King. He ordered the monastery burned to the ground along with all the occupants in it, including the Princess. Amazingly, the Princess not only survived but rescued many from the fire, without so much as a burn on her hands. The King refused to acknowledge the miraculous escape and ordered the Princess executed. This attempt also failed, for sword after sword broke. No weapon could touch her. Then suddenly, a huge white, sacred tiger appeared and rescued the Princess, taking her to the sacred mountain known as Fragrant Mountain on the island of Putuo Shan.

The King finally realized how special his daughter was when she voluntarily provided the medicine from her own body to heal him when he became very ill. Filled with remorse, the King fell to his knees and asked for her forgiveness. To acknowledge his sincerity, he built a beautiful temple in her honor. Today the island of Putuo Shan in China is considered to be her main residence, and the whole island has been dedicated to her.

Because of her work on Earth, the Princess had not only achieved the status of a Bodhisattva, which means *"One who has achieved enlightenment"*, but she also attained the level of a Mahasattva. A Mahasattva is known as, *"One who has reached the transcendent level"*. It is a higher state of enlightenment while in human form and which is endowed with special powers, such as the ability to act beyond natural laws. Upon physical death, the Enlightened one has earned the right to enter Nirvana. Nirvana in Buddhism is the equivalent to what Christianity considers Heaven. It is believed to be a place for those who have reached enlightenment and who can now ascend into the higher realms of bliss in the presence of the Creator. Upon her death, however, as Miao-Shan stood at the threshold to Nirvana, she continued to hear the prayers and lamentations emanating from those still suffering on Earth. Her love for humanity was so great that she resolved right there and then not to enter the next level of ascension, but to remain within the boundaries of the Earth Realms so that she could continue to answer the prayers of all men and women in need.

Today she is mostly known as Quan Yin, Kwan Yin or Kuan Yin, which means *"She who hears the world's cries of pain and suffering."* Because of her heritage, she is revered in all the countries in Southeast Asia. She is considered to be the patron saint of all mothers and children. She is often painted in an androgynous form to remind everyone who prays to her that gender does not matter. Her message is that both men and women have equal rights to achieve enlightenment. She is addressed in different names in different regions of the world based upon each area's religious, customary and legendary belief systems.

In Thailand she is called KUAN IM or CHAO MAE KUAN IM

In Vietnam, QUAN AM or QUAN THE AM

In Indonesia, KWAN IM or DEVI KWAN IM or MAK KWAN IM (Mak means Mother)

In the Khmer, PREAH MAE KUN CILEM

In Japan, KANON or KANZEON or KWANNON

In Korea, GWAN EUM or GWAN SE EUM

In Hong Kong, Southern China and Macau, KUN YUM or KWUN YAM or KUN LAM

In the rest of China, pockets in Northern India and parts of Tibet, GUAN YIN or GUAN SHI YIN

In China, Guan Yin Pusa is a prayer chant that acknowledges the Goddess of Compassion and Mercy. The Pusa prayer or mantra, *"Om Mani Padme Hum"* raises the consciousness energy into opening the divine heart frequency. Words are vibrations of power, and when accompanied by sound frequencies of a song or a chant, it has an immediate effect on our energy field. Om Mani Padme Hum translated means *"the opening of the jewel in the Lotus,"* or interpreted as, *"may the heart awaken with Divine Love and may I know myself to be an awakened being of light."* When this mantra is chanted, it is a connection that reaches beyond time and space to the accumulated love and devotion of every human who has, or is chanting the prayer to the Mother Creator Goddess. It is believed that the energetic sounds of this mantra are also chanted by the celestial beings, forming a bridge for the humans choosing to enter the evolutionary path.

Because of China's long lasting policy and custom, the birth of male children was given priority and many female children were either killed or abandoned. This gave rise to another powerful Pusa, or prayer chant, that is often offered to ask for fertility in begetting male babies and protection for all children. A smaller, quick chant is *Ohm Shanti* which simply invokes peace for the Self and the world.

Statues and paintings are created to depict the various belief systems and are still held in honor and prayed to as a representation of the Goddess. She is often shown in these art forms as sitting on the left side of the Buddha as the feminine aspect of compassion, mercy, and Love. Together they portray the promise that anyone can become a Buddha, meaning that one can achieve the ultimate peace within the enlightened Self and thereby reach the level of a Bodhisattva.

In China, lotus plants grow in profusion and parts of the plant are used for healing, food and medicine. As a Goddess of healing, Kuan Yin chose the lotus blossom as a symbol of life, purity, wisdom and enlightenment. In Sanskrit, her name Quan Yin is translated as "Born of the Lotus." The interesting life cycle of the lotus closely mirrors our human life journey here on Earth, for it needs all four elements to grow. The seed has to fall down into the muddy bottom of the pond, extend a shoot through the murky waters, then burst through the surface into the light of the sun, there to bloom and display its beauty. A wise ancient sage once said, "*No mud, No lotus.*"

Some of her statues are shown as a female deity with many heads and arms. This is in line with the belief that, in order to understand and respond to the needs of so many anguished cries, the Goddess needed more body parts. At one point the lamentations were so overwhelming that it shattered her head into eleven pieces. Another Deity immediately came to help and transformed the pieces into eleven individual heads so that she could hear with more ease. The same thing happened to her arms and hands. To meet her desire to answer every prayer, she was given one thousand arms and hands that could reach more sentient beings who are suffering. The statues today however, usually only show eight arms as a representation of those one thousand arms. The Quan Yin statues, showing her holding a small jar of the healing waters of life and a sheaf of rice stalks, represent healing, fertility and new growth.

Another chapter of the legend told the story of how the Princess helped the Dragon King of the Sea. In gratitude the Dragon King sent his daughter, the Dragon Princess, to assist the Goddess. The Dragon Princess became one of her students and embraced the teachings of the Buddha and chose to become a lifelong companion to the Princess

Miao-Shan. The Goddess is the only passenger the dragon would allow to ride on her back and is so displayed in many of the art forms.

Throughout the ages, many people felt that she answered their prayers and her reputation as a Goddess, who could be approached for any kind of help, grew with time. She is known to help fishermen at sea, and is often prayed to as the Old Buddha of the South Sea, I KUAN TAO. To the misfortunate, Kuan Yin is worshipped as the Goddess to help the sick, the disabled, the poor and troubled souls.

Within Tibetan Buddhism she is worshipped as the Goddess Tara, while in Japan she is known as Tarani Bosatsu. The Tara Goddess appears in different colors to represent her different aspects. The White Tara embodies wisdom, serenity and longevity. The Green Tara is the connection to the Earth Mother and the gift to overcome obstacles. The Black Tara symbolizes power and is the guardian who wards off all evil. The Red Tara looks after enchantments, magnetic and magical powers. The Orange Tara is known as the liberator, freeing the supplicant from all levels of imprisonment. The Yellow Tara is closely linked to the Hindu Goddess Lakshmi and oversees abundance, wealth and prosperity.

Years went by, and eventually East and West intersected and met. As Christianity entered China, awareness rose within humanity, and it became apparent that there is a link between the Goddess Quan Yin and Mother Mary. Both are aspects of the Ultimate Divine Mother God and carry the same energies of the Divine Feminine. To express this awareness, there are now pictures and statues of the Goddess with a child in her arms in the same way that Mary carried the baby Jesus in her arms. Both are revered as the ultimate nurturing and loving mother image, who loves all children unconditionally.

At this point we intercept briefly and make a fast forward leap to the year 1987. We are at that pivotal time in the human journey where humanity as a whole, has to make a choice in Consciousness. The Harmonic Convergence in 1987 was just that moment in time when we, as humans, made the collective choice, the agreement to rise to another level of Mass Consciousness together. This created a great shift in mass awareness and suddenly words, such as *meditation, yoga and mantras* became the accepted norm in our society.

Today religious belief systems are being examined and questioned by many who have suddenly awakened to the idea that there is something more out there. There is awareness that all religions carry only a piece of quantum Truth and that our job is to honor all parts of this truth. This search for Universal Truth is beginning to enter the conscious mind of men. To help with this transition the Energy of the Feminine Buddha, now known to us as Quan Yin, has come into more prominence within the western world. Her name and her visage have become more familiar and recognized within our western society. Because of her position within the Earth's spiritual realms, and her promise that she will stay to help anyone who calls upon her, she was the perfect candidate to assist in the energetic Shift. She has many human helpers all over the world, and I am just one of the many. I have chosen to dedicate the rest of my life to be in complete service and support to the Goddess Quan Yin, as she dedicates her energies in complete loving service to humanity.

She embodies the energies of the Divine Mother Creator God and reinforces and stabilizes the powerful etheric gates that are now opening to allow the waves of the Divine Feminine to flow through. These waves of Unconditional Love energies are vital in balancing the male and female strands of energy within each one of us. It is a major step towards the changes necessary to facilitate the Great Shift in Consciousness, to which we have all agreed.

The following information given is a fraction of the vast tapestry of the human journey; it is only the tip of the ice-berg. There are a multitude of messengers walking the earth at this very moment and each carries a piece of the puzzle. This humongous puzzle piece of creation cannot be completed until each piece is brought home and anchored into its special spot. This requires an orchestrated teamwork based on words of light, such as Unconditional Love, cooperation, acceptance, tolerance and compassion. This is only one message, one sign post, for all those who are choosing to enter and walk the Goddess Path of transformation with the Lady Quan Yin, who holds the Goddess puzzle piece.

The Goddess often repeats her messages to get her point across. She maintains that repetition is how the human mind learns. Repeating a lesson over and over again creates and strengthens a path into the memory banks of the brain. Chanting resonating mantras are, therefore, very beneficial, as it clears a path of meditative stillness into the high mind.

She is always very gentle with me, for I am not very scientifically, technologically and mathematically knowledgeable. Her simplified version of the sequence of events has been geared to my understanding and others who are in the same mind set. For those who yearn for more technical details there are many sources available that provide more in-depth information.

PART ONE

Setting the Stage

CHAPTER ONE

Why?

I was sitting on a smooth sandy beach facing the ocean and marveling at the beauty of the vista before me. The warm sand cradled my seat and the smooth surface of an old driftwood branch supported my back, creating a very comfortable niche. The blue sky overhead was dotted with lazy drifting puffs of white clouds, and the sun was at its perfect angle and brilliance in the sky. I had not spoken, nor listened to anyone speaking to me, that required a response for three days. I was content, at peace and cocooned within my own meditative silence.

It came as a soft caressing, billowing breeze from the ocean. It was the gentlest of kisses on my cheeks and I immediately recognized the gentle loving energy of the Goddess Quan Yin. "*Shih Yin it is time*". The whisper floated around and inside me. She named me Shih Yin once I had accepted my connection with her. She told me that I am known by that name in the Goddess Realm.

Joyfully I gazed at the crashing waves, opening myself in response and anticipation of her call. Part of her essence is always with me, but at special times like this sunny day, her energetic signature would be a more powerful and overwhelming wave of love. I knew then that a major part of her Being had eased through the etheric gate, and she had an important message to impart.

Other ethereal Beings heard and answered as well, for I saw them gliding, floating and rising from the unending horizon of the ocean. They came, calmly stepping onto the warm, white sand, their feet barely touching the surface of the beach, rows of Masters, Goddesses and Angels of Light, silently gathering around me. I did not see the Goddess, but

I sensed her powerful and vast presence surrounding us all. We were gathered on a Californian beach when, suddenly the air around us seemed to shimmer and twist upon itself and I found myself standing among my ethereal companions in another space and time. We were standing on a large marble patio facing another beautiful watery expanse. I was very familiar with this scene. It was the edgeless Lotus Pond that was boundless and carpeted with multi-colored lotuses of all sizes and shapes. The same gentle breeze brought whiffs of an exotic perfume and I deeply breathed in this subtle fragrance that permeated the clear air. It immediately lifted me into a welcomed alternate state of bliss.

Again, the soft whisper entered my consciousness, "*It is time.*" I understood the cue immediately. It was time to write the words that may bring more clarity and understanding to the masses and to write the story for myself that I may enter my new beginnings.

The messages and the teachings of the Goddess could not be completed in one day, for she understood the limitations of my human form. I have, therefore, compiled the subsequent transmissions into a cohesive book-long story. To ensure the fluidity of the story I have also taken the liberty to revise a major part of her direct communication into a more narrative style. Each section is interconnected with each other and forms a chain, a link that eventually will lead to a necklace of awakening, understanding, wisdom and enlightenment.

That warm sunny day was the perfect entry for Quan Yin's powerful messages. Her beautiful presence was among us and her loving energies radiated and enveloped all those present, visible or invisible. She was dressed in a flowing gown of blues and violet with an iridescent pearlescent white under-shift that undulated in and out of her outer gown as she walked to the center of the patio. She invited us all to take a seat as she gracefully sat on a comfortable cushioned ornate stool. As always, she was the picture of serenity and loveliness. As I admired her beauty, my sight was drawn to the exquisite carving of a beautiful dragon that wound itself around the pedestal of her stool. I was startled and, somewhat humorously shocked to discover that it was alive for it winked at me as I stared at it with fascination and wonder.

The Goddess began to speak, and to my sense of hearing her voice was preceded by the chimes of crystal bells heralding a loving message to humanity. She turned and her gaze fell on me. "Shih Yin, through you," she said, "I have heard the frustration and the pain within that one questing word from our human brothers and sisters: Why?"

"With the loving energy of support from all of us here we will answer the question in such a manner that it may bring peace in the hearts of those who are ready to listen and awaken."

She continued as she looked not only at all those present, but it seemed as if she was also addressing another audience beyond. "I hereby invoke and enhance the wonderful gift that all humans possess, the gift of the power of the imagination. All beings love stories and many have gained deeper understanding and wisdom with the fairy tales, legends and parables. I ask that you open your mind to the gift of the imagination, wonder and curiosity of the child."

"Imagine a world inhabited only by people who love to cook. It is a country of cooks and chefs where everyone is happily creating new recipes, using every ingredient available. Each new variation of cake, soup, stew, salad, jam or pickle is shared readily with everyone and stored within the mainframe of the massive Mother Computer of the world.

"Then one day, to everyone's astonishment, there is not a single new ingredient to be found anywhere. No new recipe can be recorded and the creative waves became stagnant. Everything comes to a halt, a standstill with no new creative action possible.

"The governing council immediately took action and authorized a massive search. The call went out to the Universe itself and the search began. Then, waves of joy and excitement rippled through the realm. A new component, a new discovery, was found in an obscure, faraway place. It was located in an area previously undiscovered. The signature frequency of this new source was detected by the searching scientific explorers.

"A team was quickly organized and was overseen by seven directors. Immediately the expedition was underway to identify the place and the new substance. The team soon realized that it was a very hazardous and strange journey. The destination could only be reached by entering a dark cave that extended into a dark tunnel and finally ended before a very narrow dark hole. It was a deep and narrow mineshaft. The exploring engineers had lowered a flashlight into the shaft and discovered that it was so deep that the light eventually disappeared from sight. It was a place of desolation where the beam of a flashlight could not penetrate the depth of the thick darkness."

The Goddess had me mesmerized by the story as I easily identified myself as part of the exploratory team. Waves of excited anticipation wove itself around the audience which included me. I felt such a sense of gratitude and honor that I was invited to be a part of this gathering.

"The team had many questions and concerns for the investigators, scientists and engineers who were present," Quan Yin continued, "It is too narrow for anybody to enter the shaft. How do we get down there? How deep do we have to go? How much power do we need? How is it to be mined? What tools do we need? How can the miners exist without light? How long will this take? They need help; you cannot send them there alone. Can it be done?"

"All the questions and concerns were put on the table before the council, and the laborious planning began. First on the agenda was a call for volunteers and they came from every corner of the country. It was explained to them how dangerous this mission was and that there was no guarantee that they would come back in one piece. They would be forever changed by the experience but at the same time honored beyond measure for what they would be able to bring back home. The adventurous and courageous ones stepped bravely forward with full knowledge of the hazards and the dangers of the mission. They were all chosen because they were the best qualified to face this incredible journey into the unknown.

"Because it was such a narrow shaft, each volunteer had to agree to give part of his/her DNA to be grown into a miniature self that could fit into the shaft. With everyone's agreement the scientists went to work and began to create an army of miniature mining explorers. We have decided to name these volunteer particles Mini Miners, in short Minis. In a way, the donating volunteers became the parents, the source of the existence of the Minis. As a starting incentive, the seven counseling directors pledged their complete support and their personal resources to assist with this massive expedition.

"Special tools and equipment were needed but the most important factor was a special suit that was essential not only to allow the Minis to enter such a narrow shaft but also to protect them. A special long cable had to be manufactured as well to be used as a silvery lifeline that was to be permanently attached to each explorer as they were being lowered into the shaft. Specific vehicles for transportation had to be built to facilitate the exploration of as wide of an area as possible.

"Each would also be equipped with a special seed of light that was surgically inserted in the heart so that it will never go out. It was hoped that the numerous light droplets sent this way could eventually penetrate the darkness below so that everyone could see what was hidden there. Silver cord was used to create the line because it could reflect the presence of light and it was a means for the support team to keep track of their mate."

As we sat rapt with attention, the Goddess continued with her magical story. Protrusions and ledges were discovered along the upper portion of the shaft that were big enough for relay stations to be established there to house the support teams. Each miner would have its own support team that would consist of the one whose DNA they shared. Therefore twelve more miniatures were created to form this special group for the one who would be lowered to the very bottom of the shaft. All Mini team members were connected with the silver lifeline that would also serve as a communication line and a reminder that they were not alone.

A different type of communication frequency channel had to be formulated because of the remote location and the depth of the shaft. Regular radio frequencies would not work for this amazing project for it could not be intercepted, or received by the miniscule Miners. The scientists went to work again and came up with a very unusual solution. The volunteer parents were asked to fall into a deep trans-sleep pattern and enter the land of dreams. From this platform they were able to perceive the miniscule, fine gossamer strands of transmissions, monitor and receive instant data that could then be relayed to the Mother Computer for analysis and evaluation.

Preparations were soon underway and security measures were implemented by volunteer security teams. The scientific and engineering group agreed to continue their support by staying at the entrance of the cave to monitor the progression of the mission. Every imaginable supply that would be needed was sent down to ensure the survival of the Minis and the journey began.

Various groups were lowered with the intent to explore different sections of the perimeter of the area that each would reach. The main expedition, however, was comprised of the largest company and their job was to collect and send feedback information to the closest monitoring station. At first, this company reached an area they thought to be the bottom of the shaft but soon realized that they had only reached a large ledge. From this location they could still see the lights of the monitoring station and their individual lights could give enough illumination to search the area. Although they discovered some unusual specimens, they were not able to process the raw material, and the team was pulled back up for a rest and a restructuring session.

The silver cord needed to be lengthened and strengthened to reach the deeper layers below, and for a period of time, different teams were sent back lower and lower into the dark depths. This continued until one day when a group yelled out in surprise for they found themselves falling into a pool of sticky and oily dark fluid. It was a deep pit filled with a tar-like substance, and it was as if they had found a rich vein of crude oil for the very first time. They were exuberant, realizing that they had finally reached their destination which was the central core of the mine. With joy they wallowed, rolled and played in this raw material that was filled with potentials of what they could create with it.

The next step would be to discover how to refine, transform and change the dark oil into numerous products. Imagine processing, refining and transforming it into products like gasoline, Vaseline, soap, perfume and even edible products. The problem was that no refinery could be built within the pool itself. This potential problem had been anticipated, and the Minis received the message to enter a specific code inside their heart to activate the special laboratory there. However, this directive was blocked by the dark goo and not received; thus, it could not be accessed and implemented. What was not quite anticipated was that the dark substance clung like glue to anyone who entered it. Soon, it coated everything, including the heart chamber containing the light-seed. The monitoring teams at the stations were faced with another challenge when suddenly they could no longer detect the light sparks below, thus terminating the communication links. They tried to rescue and pull everyone back up, but, surprisingly found resistance from the Minis. It took a lot of effort, but the engineering teams were finally able to draw everyone back to recuperate at the rest stations on the shaft's ledges.

The findings were analyzed by the council, and it was concluded that the miners had been lowered too fast and were not prepared for what they encountered. They were like children who suddenly found themselves in a room filled with all kinds of new, intriguing treats and toys. They submerged themselves with abandon and indulged and gorged themselves. Not only did they get sick, but in the process, forgot why they were there and what their assignments were.

New teams were formed. This time, the descending journey of every team into the dark pool was monitored and stabilized by the technicians on the stations above. Safety features were added to ensure that the communication links would remain open. In addition, it was agreed to drill and bore parallel shafts beside the main shaft to allow other teams access as observers and potential rescuers in case of emergencies. These team members did not have the Mini-miner structures, but were encapsulated within more 'alien' suits and not visible to the regular miner population.

Quan Yin paused and her gentle, loving gaze touched every attentive face around her. "Keep this scenery, this analogy in your mind," She continued, "I invite you to open your imagination even further as I superimpose another story over the one you just heard. We will refer back to the Mini Miner story whenever necessary to provide more clarity."

"Breathe in the presence of the Ultimate Source of Consciousness, known to many as the Alpha and the Omega. As you know, that Source is known by many names. To keep the flow of this story, I will address it as God, the All That Is, and The Creator of All Things. God is the eternal, infinite source of pure light, the embodiment of Unconditional Divine Love energy, and the ultimate source of unlimited Unity Consciousness. At one point in the reality of its Being, God wanted to know itself and to experience its inner Self. It turned inward, and this creative twist created the template of the Infinity symbol, you know as the figure 8. Then the Creator of All That Is, spoke with joy the words, *"I AM,"* and the first creation manifested in multiple sparks of Light. It was the ultimate Big Bang of Creation."

This version of the ageless story of Creation resonated with me and gave me a deeper understanding and awareness of our beginnings. We are the Sparks, the baby Godlings, the offspring of Divine Father-Mother God created in Its Holy image the instant that the power lines intersected to create the figure eight. Light is the ultimate frequency of love, and we are all particles of It; the complete duplicates of the Creator God. We are all brothers and sisters of one big Divine Family and like each baby born into a family, we are unique individuals carrying the same God-cell DNA structure of our parents.

The Creator rejoiced and experienced itself through each one of Its children. "Go forth", the Father-Mother said lovingly. "Play, create and share all your experiences with me." And we did. We, the Godlings, created stars, universes, omniverses and dimensional realities which became our playground. In human terms we played for a very long time, for time does not exist in the realm of Love and Light. Then just like the story that was told earlier, there came a standstill, a kind of gridlock of creative energy. There was limitless, unrealized and unmanifested potentiality, but it needed a new shift of energy. An injection of a new formula was needed so that it could be woven into a second creation within the tapestry of Divine Unity Consciousness. In other words, we wanted to create a new playground.

Something needed to be done to start the next creation, and in order to do that, a new energetic signature needed to be found. It was quickly found, but could only be harvested and processed in a much lower dimensional frequency known as the third dimension. It was very far down the dimensional chasm and referred to as the void of darkness, a dense layer of shadows that was always there. Yet, no one had as yet explored and examined its raw, untapped potentiality. It was a region of the total absence of Light particles.

Representatives of all the realities came and a group of seven council members were chosen to head the infrastructure needed for this exciting project. These members were known as the Elohim, the beings of the highest frequencies of light. A physical platform of dense matter was needed as a game board, and the Elohim chose the location within the three-dimensional reality to manifest this space. A small blue planet revolving in this density was created in a corner of a remote galaxy to anchor the space required for this new adventure. At its birth, the Earth was a ball of swirling light energy that was refracted into lower vibrational frequencies and slowly coalesced, evolving into matter. Within this reality ran the currents of *Duality*, which is a state of awareness of opposing forces of dark and light, such as right and wrong, sweet and bitter, good and evil, and life and death.

Gaia, an entity of great light offered to embody the physical manifestation called Earth with her essence. She became the living guardian and host of everything on, and in it, embracing the role of the Earth Mother. Linear time and space were interwoven into the Earth's three dimensional template and put in place as boundaries of a Duality containment field. The Earth's rotation around the sun gave rise to the concept of day and night. The sun's warmth and light nurtured and nourished the Earth, while the moon reigned at night, influencing the tides within and without every creature living upon the Earth. The four elements manifested, stabilizing this structure. Within the human perspective of time, the process of completing this reality took millions of Earth years. To appease the human limited, enquiring mind it became a legendary story told as the Seven Days of Creation. As part of her living essence, other supporting energies were created within the four elements as the plant, mineral, water, air and animal kingdoms. The stage was now set and everything was in place to support the arrival of the main players.

The call went out to all directions of the Omniverse for volunteers from different realms of existence. It was answered, and many came from multiple dimensional directions. It is important to understand that we were, in human terms, huge Beings of Light that had only played and lived within the highest frequencies of light. The entrance into the third dimensional reality was like that narrow, dark shaft in the other story line and it took many engineers and scientists to figure out how to make this journey work. Imagine that you had to pour a lake into one small bottle, because the small bottle is the only thing that could go through the narrow hole in this shaft.

Every volunteer received the same briefing before they were selected and chosen for this special mission. It was a challenging journey of exploration into the unknown dark void of unrealized and untapped potentialities. They all knew that they would be forever changed and that there was no going back until the mission was completed. In addition, the awareness of Self and the connection to Source would be hidden from the primary Soul, the one who would do all the work while wearing the mantle, the space-suit, the costume of a human.

Constant assistant and support were essential to the success of the mission and a very special monitoring and rescue grid was created and stationed at the dimensional borders. Each traveller was asked to donate a special drop of their Spirit-essence, to form a pool of combined energetic substances. This mixture ensured, and established, a unique link of consciousness from the higher vibrational realities to each human-Soul construct. It was used to create the first occupants of a major support relay hub. The new personnel were given the status of Archangels. The four main ones were Michael, Raphael, Gabriel and Uriel. Although connected as One, each had a unique, individual personality and had his own expertise to offer. It was mutually agreed that Michael was chosen to be the department supervisor over the whole company of assisting Angelic Beings, in total service to the journey of the Soul. As the project evolved, this group would eventually be joined by the company of Ascended Masters, and other interested parties from the higher realms of existence."

Quan Yin paused, dazzling us with her beautiful countenance, then continued with her magical tale. She explained that the analogy of the small bottle then, is the same as the Mini Miner story, except that in this version it is called the human vessel. Each human vessel contains the same GOD DNA cell from the Light Being who volunteered for this mission. The scientists then developed something called adamantine particles that contain carbon molecules to lower its frequency matching the vibration of the third dimension. This mix also contained the substance that was used in creating the backdrop for this three-dimensional stage. A universe was created filled with a galaxy of stars, including the sun and the Earth itself, and it became the base foundation for the human structure. It is a construct of living essences similar to that of the animals and the plants. The only difference is that the human form is a receptacle for the Soul particle and contains the potential of higher intelligence and awareness of Self. The first prototype of the human host, the human vessel, was finally ready. It was a very small container when viewed by the enormous Beings of Light, but the model was equipped with numerous sophisticated electromagnetic mechanisms. Imagine a walking, talking bio-based, elaborate and independent robotic, computer system linked to a massive and powerful Mother-board, with an unlimited, eternal power source.

The next step was for each participant to donate and release another drop of its Spirit-light, its etheric essence that could fit into the small vessel. Remember that we were beings of great balls of light existing in the higher frequencies of consciousness. Therefore, each drop had to be lowered through multiple dimensional veils before it could occupy the human vessel. Twelve drops of light were assigned as members of a support team to the one who would enter the final destination in the lower and denser space of matter. The droplets were identified as Soul parts and had to be refracted through the crystalline layers of each dimensional veil in order to reach compatibility with their final destination, *the reality of Duality*. They have become the Mini Miners of the earlier analogy.

In the same vein, the Spirit-Light-Source also had to enter the dream world in order to keep an open communication frequency with all the Soul members of the team. In other words Spirit went into deep meditative sleep state to begin **the dream of the Soul**. To prevent contamination and distractions, another element was implemented before the departure of the teams. The last Soul-drop would be **blinded,** meaning that all memory of its source would be completely hidden from its awareness the moment it merged with biology. To ensure that they would have continual support and assistance, each Soul-drop would be accompanied by one or two Spirit-Souls we know as guardian angels, as they are birthed into the human vessels. The Guardian Angels, or guides, would whisper encouragements, provide gentle guidance and, at the same time, monitor the Soul's journey. These Spirit-Angels are sometimes departed family members, or other Soul connections, who have offered to take the position of Spirit-etheric-guides for each specific life time.

Before departure, the Soul was finally given a present in the form of a tool box to use on its journey. *Free Will* was one of the special tools, and with it, every choice would be honored, without penalties or judgements from anyone. In the tool box were also keys to open many files when the soul is ready to use the information during its sojourn on the earth plane. Unique Soul properties were also kept in this box for the Soul to use at the appropriate time of growth. The Soul-sparks are like children who are sent to school starting with kindergarten, and given their first school kit to explore. As they grow older, they will need different items to help them learn and navigate maturity. The same theory applies to the Soul-human spark.

The stage was set, and the start button was activated. The chosen Soul-drops began the downward journey and refracted slowly through each layer. As the team descended, each member of the team would anchor itself on a different dimensional platform creating a ladder, a relay station of support, recognized as the Higher-Soul-Selves. The one that was stationed at the top of the dimensional ladder was deemed the *Over-Soul* and held the direct line of communication to Its Source. This connecting bridge allowed the Soul to be the scientist, the experiment, and the observer, all at the same time.

To help us gain a better grasp of the Soul story, the Goddess encouraged us to refer back to the Mini Miner story line, as we hung on to her every word. Continuing, she went on to explain how the Over-Souls were in turn connected to the angelic realms manned by the Archangels and their choir of angels. The Archangels were the direct link to frequencies of the Ultimate Source, the Creator God Consciousness. Imagine this structure as the long-distance phone lines on Earth where you can call and talk to anyone anywhere in the world. The trick is to find the right phone frequency, the right language of communication, and of course, having the resources to pay for it. In this case, the resources would be the right energetic frequency, the compatibility and acceptance of the human-Soul that this line exists.

Finally, the last Soul-drop refracted through the three dimensional veil flowing gently into the waiting vessel and immediately bound itself into a ***symbiotic relationship*** with the human body. It went through the process of metempsychosis, a process where the soul particles merged with biology. Each Soul carried the drop of light, the eternal God-Spark within itself, and as part of the merge, anchored this seed of light within the heart of its human host for safe keeping during its journey.

Light particles are weightless, therefore to remain in the heaviness of matter; it needed to be anchored permanently in the physical body to allow the symbiotic relationship to work. It would be similar to a boat that has to drop anchor to remain in the harbor. Upon the final entry into density, the Soul refracted its essence into the seven rays of creation, each a different color frequency. It became the sophisticated electromagnetic seven chakra wheels rooted in the etheric spinal column of the human body. These seven rays of creation are the lowest frequencies of an extensive column of multiple vibrational creative rays and came from the drawing board of the seven Elohim.

The chakras became the junction points between Soul and biology. This configuration allows the Soul to experience, not only physical growth, but every thought, every emotion and all biological functions of the physical and etheric body layers. These are also recognized as the subtle bodies. Etheric space is the medium that exists in between the particles of matter and is considered to be the area in space through which electromagnetic waves are transmitted. The seven subtle body layers of the physical body exist within this etheric space and are therefore not always seen by human physical sight.

For further protection against the inter-dimensional shifts, the physical human structure is encapsulated within an energetic *spacesuit*. It cocoons the physical and the subtle etheric bodies. The subtle seven layers are projections of the chakra colors and form a pulsing energetic field that can now be seen by some humans as the auric field. These pulsing, etheric bodies are further encapsulated within a golden egg-shaped field coined the *Golden Egg*. Another intricate geometric structure called the *Merkabah* spins around the capsule ensuring more protection for the Soul. The ancient word, Merkabah, roughly means rotating, spiralling fields of light particles forming the light body vehicle. It has many layers of what is now considered *sacred geometric* shapes in the form of pyramids of multiple facets. The whole structure is similar to a gyroscope, where the Golden Egg shape is the still point center that is surrounded by spinning, rotating fields of geometric shaped energy fields. The pyramid shapes are spinning prisms, interconnected with the chakra system and correlated to vibration of the five elements. More information about the structures and the functions of the light-vehicle would be given later, in conjunction with the rewiring process.

Besides human habitation, there are many other entities that co-exist within the multiple realities occupying the same space within the Earth's realms. These are the various Elemental Kingdoms such as the Elven Kingdoms, the Little People and other Fairy Kingdoms. They live within other dimensional layers of the Earth and are only visible to those who resonate with their vibrational frequencies of existence. Each has its own experiences of evolvement and their story waits to be told at another time.

CHAPTER TWO

The Soul's Earth Adventures.

The Goddess explained that the ingredient, the component that was to be harvested, that new potentiality, is the final product of the process of transforming the dark, negative and heavy emotions of fear, such as anger, pain, suffering, and revenge, into the higher frequencies of light. These include forgiveness and gratitude. Imagine mining a piece of dirty-looking rock and transforming it into a precious diamond that can reflect brilliant beams of light. Referring back to the Mini Miner's tale, think of it as the mining of the crude oil and refining it into golden gasoline, or fragrant perfumes and soaps.

The refining tools were stored within the Mini Miner bodies, and similarly, the process of purification and metamorphosis can only happen within all the layers of the human structure. It is the highest and most intricate form of chemical alchemy that involves transmuting every component all the way to its subatomic particles. For example, as a person releases his/her anger with forgiveness, the energy is transformed into a higher frequency and is absorbed and internalized by the atomic cellular layers. Imagine, therefore, the human host as an extraordinary laboratory with the most advanced technological equipment possible and the inhabiting soul playing the role as the experiment, the scientist and the observer, all at once.

Like any experiment, there were many ups and downs and retrials before a satisfactory system was reached. One of the earliest human constructs was a taller, thinner and more flexible human frame work. This group chose to live within the ancient Earth areas known as Mu and later evolved into Lemuria. This scenario did not meet the hopeful results that the higher monitoring hierarchy had desired.

The Lemurian human contained too much of the '*light*' component thus causing an imbalance within the structural framework. They could not completely embrace and descend into the quagmire of the muddy thickness of the dark energies such, as violence, animosity, jealousy, fear and hatred. In other words, the percentage of love energy within the Soul was higher than expected, creating disharmony with its biological host. The Duality principle could not root itself completely when the Lemurian simply would not choose to experience the energy of hatred, for instance. Therefore they were unable to grasp the transformative components of forgiveness and acceptance.

It was decided to abort this particular mission. The Souls were re-called and returned to home base, back to the drawing board. A new set of parameters were put into play for the next group known as Atlanteans, who occupied the ancient lands of Atlantis. Atlantis flourished, and for a while, there was great anticipation of the possibility for manifestation of the potentiality of transformation.

Atlantis was created to support a high level of Consciousness, and it rose in direct correlation with the sophisticated technology made available to the public. As time went by, two distinct factions began to emerge within this society. One was known as the Sons of One, a group who held on to the memory of Oneness of Source, and the ultimate Unity Consciousness of the High Mind. The other group began to call themselves the Sons of Belial. This group chose to plunge deeply into the darker emotional pits within the human mind. They chose to mine and explore the gratifications of the human senses, particularly within the range of sexual stimuli. This faction grew rapidly and soon became the majority within the masses, plunging the world deeper into the energies of Duality.

This mass focus on the darker energies gave birth to the vibrational manifestation referred to as *Evil*, the embodiment of which was labelled as *Satan* or even *Lucifer.* Lucifer was the Archangel who volunteered to carry the burden of anchoring the dark strands in this realm until it all could be transformed and refined. In a way, Lucifer was the angel who carried the first cross for all of us. There was now a distinct awareness of the meaning of dark and light, black and white, good and evil, ugly and beautiful, and so on. Fear was now firmly anchored in the hearts of men and permeated every corner of the world, saturating, and infusing the earth and its four elements with the darkness of violent emotions. Unconditional Divine Love, the Energy of Light, seemed to dim, flicker and to disappear from the world.

The downward slide into Duality continued to gain momentum. The knowledge of advanced technology was channelled into the production of cloned personnel. Clones were not considered human and were categorized as mindless slaves, as worker ants who had no rights. They were allotted the menial, dirty and even dangerous jobs in the mines. Friendships and loving relationships were forbidden. They could never marry, have a family, or even have children. Severe punishments and torture were inflicted upon any who were caught violating any of the laws. Within these Souls were stamped and recorded the most painful experiences of the dark energies of suffering. This untransformed energy created heavy group karma and was dutifully recorded in the Akashic Hall of Records, which is situated within a dimensional plateau in the Earth Realm. All files recorded within the hall are known as the Akash.

From a human perspective, Atlantis was at its highest peak of prosperity and wealth. Crystal technology generated almost unlimited power and was used for practically everything. Energy was used indiscriminately, from powering their luxurious homes to operating construction tools. It was also used for running transportation vehicles on the ground and gliding flitters in the air. Laser technology was used similarly to what we have today in our communication systems and was used in the medical field. Rejuvenation and regeneration options were available for the rich and the wealthy of society. The chasm between the poor and the wealthy became deeper and wider. The energies of Suffering and Survival gained a firmer hold in the human construct, deeply rooted within the first Chakra.

This rapid descent into the turbulent three dimensional densities began to take its toll. The dive into Duality and the blatant abuse of the energy fields were too fast and were getting out of control. The discovery of how to manufacture explosive devices only increased the fascination of violence. The relationship with Gaia, the Earth Mother, deteriorated. Fear of Nature, such as the presence of wild roaming animals, mushroomed, and the wild hunt became part of human entertainment.

Human errors, miscalculations, and rising tempers fuelled by Ego-driven choices were escalating and causing major accidents everywhere. Violence erupted within many pockets of the vast empire.

As stated earlier, human biology and every living thing upon Gaia's breast are intricately connected, and the Earth began to respond to the wrenching effect of the imbalance that was created. The boiling dark cloud of discontent, fear and anger spewed out into the environment. The Earth reacted and screamed in protest, enhancing and thickening the strands of fear.

For hundreds of years, the lands heaved, volcanoes erupted, and violent storms raged around the world. The last Atlantean governing council knew that the end was near and made the decision to bury and hide many of the enormous Crystal power centers in different areas of the land. It is believed that the phenomenon of the Bermuda triangle is one of the hiding places for a number of crystalline structures hidden in the ocean depths.

Slowly Atlantis crumbled beneath the onslaught, and finally the last remnants of the great continent sank beneath the waves to be purified and kept in waiting slumber for the call to rise once more. There was a promise that many of the Souls who played a major role in this project would reincarnate again at the proper time when conditions would be favourable for the resurgence of the potential for transformation. There would be a time again when the energies of a fertile field within the Mass Consciousness could emerge to support the awakening of the Soul into full awareness.

Not everyone perished with Atlantis. There were remnants of high mountain ridges that formed new continents and fertile land masses where numerous survivors settled and evolved into different societies. Many groups escaped the onslaught and migrated to other areas of the globe today, known as South and Central America, Southern Europe and Egypt.

The Goddess paused and seemed to reflect for a moment before she continued her narrative. Every time we met for another gathering, I had the awareness that there were more and more beings that came to listen to her story. It was the strangest sensation of being in a large crowd, and yet at the same moment, I felt as if the Goddess and I were sitting alone sipping a cup of tea.

With a soft sigh, Lady Quan Yin turned to me and continued her story. "We must interject some additional information at this juncture of our tale. This knowledge was sent before, and here we would like to add more clarity to it". I heard an added loving gentleness in her voice, as if she wanted to soften the impact of the information she was about to share.

"There were many areas upon the Earth's mantle that were seeded with different life forms as part of the grand plan", she informed us. "These life forms had not yet evolved into the full human physical forms of the Atlanteans. These were Souls who had volunteered to experience the evolution of biology embodied within other earthen life forms."

The story continued with the long lost history of ancient Earth. The animal, the plant, the mineral, the air and water kingdoms were gifts from the Earth Mother. All were created to ensure and support the survival of human life on the planet. One Soul group opted to enter and merge its essence with the various kingdoms to experience its different structural life forms. Thus, the presence of mythical beings—such as centaurs, harpies, gryphons and mermaids—entered human mythology. Linear time marched on, and this Soul group began to mutate into more human-like beings. It was a slow process and not many survived this experiment within the energies of density.

Everything the Soul-drop experienced upon the Earth Realms were recorded in the Akash and shared within the Mass Consciousness. It is evident today within some belief systems on Earth that a person could reincarnate as a lower animal life form if that human persists in acting at a lower level of Consciousness, in other words not leading a good life. This belief is a residue of that experiment and is no longer on the list of experimentation and study. However, the knowledge to enter and journey with an animal species is available from the Akashic ledgers and has been tapped by many Shamans and Spiritual Masters. They are those who have reached the ability of astral travel and of merging their Spirit-Essence with the lower animal-awareness levels.

Animals are living essences and were created as a living survival support group. All species have survival awareness, but many have an intelligence strand that allows them to communicate with the humans at a certain resonating frequency. The main assignments for some were to provide food and to provide the lessons of Unconditional Love and awareness of nature's beauty. The human vehicle bears the same matrix as the animal form, but has an overlay of a more intricate wiring system providing a home for the Soul-drop. Once the Soul-human symbiotic partnership is in place, the Soul has the choice to share some of its love-component with a pet of its choice. The pet is then forever linked with the owner-Soul and at times, will reincarnate with the Soul, or come back for the Soul if it dies before the human vessel does. The intense grief that an owner of a pet may feel upon the death of a pet is therefore understandable, as the pet carries part of the Soul-essence.

After this particular life-form experimental event was terminated, a small number did survive for a period of time and were living in the region known as Egypt. They were in an in-between stage where they still had animal like appendages on their human physical structure. The Souls inhabiting them wanted to experience this particular stage of transformation and evolution of biology.

After the devastation, a large contingent of high ranking Atlantean refugees chose to settle in Egypt and to their surprise, encountered a strange flourishing society. They discovered that many of the local people were humanoid beings who still had tails, or feathers and fur, on their arms and legs. Some even had beak-like faces or clawed feet. It was extremely distressing to the new arrivals, especially the priests and scientists.

The Atlanteans brought their vast knowledge of technology, astronomy, anatomy and healing with them, overwhelming the local residents. The Egyptians were in awe of these magical beings, assuming that they descended into their midst from the heavens and began to worship them as Gods.

Many members of this particular Atlantean refugee group were powerful priests, healers and technicians. They immediately took steps to remedy what to them, was an abomination and began to alter the existing cultural structure to meet their needs and expectations. Their initial goal was to recreate another Atlantis, and using their advanced technology, they started to build a number of pyramids. Some of these structures were designed to harvest cosmic energies the way it was utilized in Atlantis and were constructed in perfect alignment with specific star systems in the night sky. Others were healing centers for rejuvenation, regeneration and medical facilities, where multiple operations were performed to remove the animal-like appendages. Knowledgeable surgeons initiated the program of altering the physical structure of those who still had strange body parts and successfully eradicated the offending gene for future generations.

One very powerful priest was *Ra,* and the native population began to worship him as one of their Gods. He was considered more powerful than the King himself. *Ra* prolonged his life by entering the Pyramid of Rejuvenation and was looked upon as eternal by his subsequent congregation. His knowledge and awareness of the higher state of Consciousness were such that he was considered to be '*All—Seeing*' and was being portrayed as the one '*eye*' of knowingness. The '*EYE of RA*" became a symbol of his seemingly God-like qualities. Many believed that having the Eye of RA turned to you was considered to be a holy blessing from God.

To preserve their esoteric knowledge of the Universe, the Altanteans built the first mystery schools in this new land. An intensive curriculum was offered to anyone who was gifted and interested in the mystical secrets of the Heavens. Word spread far and wide, and as a result of the school's reputation, many candidates travelled from other lands to try to gain entry as students. Thousands of years later, one student by the name of Jeshua Ben Joseph, or Jesus of Nazareth, came to learn and grow into his awakening process, as he prepared for his destiny.

These original Atlantean refugees believed that Ra could help them to recreate, rebuild and restore the Atlantis they lost. It was not to be, as hard as they tried. The energetic imbalance was too deep, the chasm too wide. As time marched on, many began to intermarry and their offspring developed their own interpretations of history and a new belief system emerged.

Before the cataclysms occurred in Atlantis the governing council agreed to try to save, and hide some of their more powerful pyramidal power centres in different parts of the country. Ra and his fellow priests made the same decision to preserve their knowledge and hid their records in a time capsule. It was hidden in a warded secret chamber under the paw of one of the sphinx guardian statues, stationed before a pyramid. They knew that their era was ending. They buried this treasure of hope with the promise that there will come a time in human history where the frequency of consciousness will rise again. It was a hope chest filled with their knowledge of failures and successes that they hoped would bring clarity and wisdom to the generations to come. The land responded to the shift in consciousness, and the changing winds turned the once fertile land into a dessert. Sand dunes flowed and buried the last remnants of Atlantis. The memories of that vast civilization disappeared from the minds of the majority of men. Tendrils of it were kept alive however, in the memories of certain souls like Plato, one of the early philosophers, and later through the channelled messages given by others such as Edgar Cayce, the Sleeping Prophet.

A Soul agreement was reached between all concerned to allow a new start and to slow down the erratic swing of the pendulum within the three dimensional reality. The Earth continued to spin, and the world of human-soul adventures proceeded to turn with the ages of men. Slowly, the knowledge of many of the higher subject matter such as advanced crystalline technology that was taken for granted in Atlantis disappeared from the Mass Consciousness Mind. Only with time were small pockets allowed to peek through, like tiny flickering candles in different areas of the world.

There was another factor that had to be taken into account at this point. When the Sons-of-Belial made their move into the world of men, they created a dark energy flow mired in Duality and attracted the warrior male energies. The gentler, nurturing Divine Feminine energies agreed to take a step back, to take a secondary role until such time when the balance needed to be restored again. By giving the male energies the upper hand, it would give the Soul a greater opportunity to explore the warrior aspect which was perceived as the heavier and darker side of Duality. Thus, the Divine Energy of the Mother Creator went into waiting slumber. However, some of the Souls who embody aspects of the Divine Feminine chose to remain within the Earth realms to continue to provide assistance. Among these are the Ascended Masters known as Quan Yin, Mary the Holy Mother, Lakshmi an Indian Goddess, and many more.

As planned, the Souls re-entered with a different set of tools and began to experience the Stone Age in different parts of the Earth, followed by the Bronze Ages of metals. Human Consciousness was given a new start, and it rose slowly in direct correlation with the rise of technology in the human intelligence. The devastation and abortion of the Atlantean era was not repeated again until the final deciding vote towards completion of the exploration was reached. When the influx of darkness caused an imbalance again in certain regions of the Earth it was dealt with accordingly. This was evident with the cleansing of Noah's flood and the burning of Sodom and Gomorrah.

The Soul's Earth adventures continued through the ages of men until such time that human Consciousness had reached a level of awakening that may promote mass enlightenment. Within the Earth's linear time-line it was predicted that this could happen in the twentieth century. In anticipation of this possibility, an infusion of higher knowledge was brought by a number of advanced Souls such as Jesus, Mohammed and the Buddha. Jesus came in to begin the 2000 year starting line within the linear Earth-time period to stimulate the energies of hope and love of one's fellow-man.

CHAPTER THREE

Reincarnation, the Karmic Wheel and The Akashic Hall of Records

In the eyes of the Creator, everything happens in an instant, in one inhaling or exhaling breath, as time does not exist within the eternal Awareness of All That Is. Within the Universal Mind of God, there are no mistakes and all human events, circumstances, situations or relationship issues are unfolding in perfect timing within the intelligence of the Divine Plan. However, for the Soul-human it became a history of life time after life time of trial and error. The Soul-human has as yet to grasp the fact that the human vehicle was created as the most perfect imperfection vessel possible. This perfect cosmic project would develop and run on its linear time schedule, in direct correspondence with the Soul-human journey of experiences on the Earth plane.

A type of a governing council with all its departments was established, not only to analyze the data accumulated, but also to monitor the progression of Soul—human Consciousness. Reincarnation was put into play right from the beginning. Everyone agreed that the lessons could not be learned and wisdom gained within one human life time. All creatures on earth are living energy constructs, created to exist within the boundaries of linear time and three-dimensional space with the attributes of a beginning, middle and an end. The human life cycle follows this pattern, and the human physical body deteriorates with age and finally releases its physical energy back to the earth. The phrase *"from dust to dust"* gives more clarity to this law of mortality in nature.

The Soul, on the other hand, is a part of an immortal, inter-dimensional Light Being and has to vacate its human host at the end of the human life-cycle. Imagine owning a car that has the most powerful and sophisticated computer monitored engine. It is very much *alive* for it has all the parts necessary to make it go; all it needs is a driver. The driver is the one who can start the car and drive it anywhere he/she wants to go. However, eventually the car will begin to break down with age, especially if it has not been looked after. A car needs regular maintenance, such as checking the fuel lines, changing the oil regularly, washing and polishing the body and replacing broken engine parts or tires. After many years of service, there comes a time when it will no longer function. The driver has to release it and begin looking for a new car. The same scenario happens with a human-Soul structure. When the Soul lets go of its human vessel, it takes all the data from all the experiences in that life-time which then becomes a file for the next incarnation. Think of it as downloading onto a disk the experiences of all your travels and adventures you had with your car, and also all the technical ups and downs. Then when you order a new car, you have all this data transferred into the new computer navigation system.

Unlike a car, however, the human vehicle has a biologically living computer system called a brain, an intelligent mind that is capable of communicating and adjusting its daily functions in cooperation with the Soul. There are times within this life journey where the Soul realizes that it is not compatible any longer with its human host and may choose to leave. When this happens, the human body will continue to *live* for a short period of time because it is living energy. However, it cannot survive without the presence of the Soul. A driver can leave the car with the engine running on automatic. It will keep running and running but eventually ceases to function as it runs out of fuel. Ultimately, the car turns to rust and no one can drive it any longer. There are numerous opportunities for the Soul to change its mind, and it is given these choices at specific times during its human journey. The Soul recognizes these time slots as *exit points,* a chance for a quick evaluation of its human situation and a choice to continue its mission or to return to the Spirit Realm. Each exit point has a story to tell, and we will leave those for another time.

To monitor the coming-and-going of the Soul into human vessels, a Karmic council has kept a ledger, keeping track of each life time. The ledgers, or Akash, are stored in crystalline form within a space called the

Akashic Hall of Records. It is situated in a dimensional reality on the Earth plane and is maintained and guarded by a Custodian.

Karma is a record of a person's life history accumulated from incarnation to incarnation. It is an accounting of every experience in a person's life time. It records everything that is said, thought, felt and done. It notes every action taken, every emotion and every response to all the senses. After each life time, each person is fully responsible for auditing his or her own recording files. At the same time, together with the Akash, it also monitors the harvesting of the transformed dark particles through a graph that shows the plusses and minuses of the combined ledgers.

To give this concept more clarity, imagine borrowing money from a bank. First you have to sign an agreement, a contract that you will pay back the principal and the interest. You know that if you cannot pay it off in one year, you negotiate an extension, fully understanding that you might have to pay more interest if you do not pay your debts on time.

The Hall of Records is like your bank, and karma is your personal payment plan. It is perceived as a wheel because it keeps rotating, turning, lifetime after lifetime until all debts are paid.

The following is an imaginary scenario for a clearer perspective. Imagine the life of a person we shall call John. John was a middle child and could not understand why his brother, Ian, was so mean to him all the time. He felt ignored, abandoned and unloved by his parents, because Ian and his sister Amy were their favorites. In his heart, he knew that he loved his family, but he struggled with anger and hatred every time he was ignored, beat up by his brother, or blamed for his sister's sneaky behaviours. John did not understand this for a long time, but after one very abusive day, with encouraging whispers of his Soul partner, he decided to forgive his parents and other members of the family. At that moment, without realizing it, John paid his dues and became free of the karmic debt he had towards his family, particularly his brother. This is where Free-Will comes into play, for no one could either force or persuade John to forgive his family completely. He was the only one who could activate this energy, using his Free-Will. He thereby transformed the energies of suffering, anger, hatred and revenge into a heart-felt peace that opened the flow of Love. With this act, John began to unveil the hidden seed of light within his heart.

The act of forgiveness is not only a trump card in the deck of the human board game, but it is the trigger point towards awareness. It has the power to wipe out the first layers of the negative column in the Akashic ledgers. John's destiny changed that day because of his choice, and he grew up with a greater potential to become a peaceful and happy man. On the other hand, his brother Ian continued his abusive behaviour unchecked, and sank deeper into the quagmire of unhappy and stressful emotions. After his death, he had to face a list of all the violent acts he had done that needed to be paid for with interest in his next life time. Ian had a choice of how he wished to pay for his actions and could script his own payment plan in his next reincarnation. If he does not succeed, and continues walking a path of darkness, his karmic debts will accumulate. Just like a bank loan, the interest will continue to rise. It is one of the reasons that some people have chosen challenging life times in order to have a chance at reducing their spiritual debt. All are held accountable for their own choices when they leave the human host behind and enter the spirit world within the earth plane. In this dimensional place, the Soul is given time, not only to heal, but also to evaluate its past journey and plan its next human life, in order to continue with the uncompleted life lessons.

Besides individual karma, there is also group, or mass karma. For instance, the choices made in Atlantis and the holocaust created a heavy karmic debt for everyone involved in those endeavours. Not only is each person responsible for his/her role in this drama, but the whole group is also held responsible. Imagine a group of people within a company that was caught embezzling from its clients. Not only will each person of the group be charged and have to face the consequences, but the whole company, must shoulder the aftermath as well. As a result, the company might lose its reputation, or in a worst case scenario declare complete bankruptcy.

The Karmic Wheel, the Akashic records, and the process of reincarnation are not easy concepts to define. They form an intricate web that connects every player in the field of the human-Soul game board. It is not possible to isolate any particular strand for the sake of examination of its energetic flow in the river of time. Every journey is planned to its minute detail, and it involves a multitude of players on the field. Imagine an actor about to perform on stage. The actor will require a team for support. He or she usually needs a partner to act out a scene. Included are the crews who look after the stage settings, the lightening, the various costumes, and the location of the stage itself. Let's not forget the script for the play where each actor must memorize his or her role and become completely immersed in the character they have chosen.

When one life is hurt, that energy reverberates throughout the whole karmic grid and affects every Soul. In the same manner, when one life is able to soar and lift itself out of the gutter, it makes every string on the web vibrate with joy.

To gain a better understanding of the Karmic Wheel, we need to look at the revolving doors of life and death within the human life cycle and the dimensional etheric layers of the Earth. Gaia, as the Earth Mother also has a chakra system and is encapsulated within numerous electromagnetic etheric fields as well. The Soul has to travel through this space to reach the first resting station with all its levels, on its way back from the Earth's physical reality.

When a human *dies,* the Soul leaves this human vehicle in almost the same manner you would leave a car that no longer works. The Soul carries with it all physical, mental and emotional memories and experiences as a downloaded disk of information. For example, when a person dies while fighting with someone and is in a state of rage, the Spirit-Soul will find itself still wrapped up in that rage when it finds itself on the other side of the Door of Death. It will need counseling, healing and a time of de-briefing and re-briefing to regain balance.

There are major levels and numerous sub-levels within this human-spirit plane, and they are within what is known as the Earth Realms. Upon exiting through the Door of Death, the Soul is met by a welcoming committee. These are not always departed family members. It depends upon the karmic luggage that the Soul is carrying at that very moment of death. The Soul-Spirit is guided to go to the Hall of Records and collect all its accumulated ledgers. (Remember the disk). This usually takes about three earth days. Unfortunately, many Soul-Spirits have linked themselves so tightly to their human life that they drown themselves in the illusion of the three dimensional life. There are many who refuse to acknowledge that they have died, and thus become the disincarnate ghosts that roam restlessly upon the Earth. Some of them even anchor themselves to a favourite item such as a house, a couch or a musical instrument.

For those who do cross over, most usually perceive the doorway as a tunnel of brilliant light and many begin to feel the energy of Divine Love enveloping their essence. Depending on their Karmic ledger, they will be greeted by one or more of their other Soul-selves, or by another group of Angelic Beings, who wear the hats of healers and counselors. It is recognized that the human journey is not an easy one, and it takes a toll on the Sprit-Soul, causing trauma within its essence. Each Soul is escorted to the corresponding platform that resonates with its frequency at the time of entry into the Spirit-Earth realms. Jesus referred to these levels when he said *"My Father has many mansions"*. Some will be gently taken to a kind of *hospital for healing* before it can continue its journey. Imagine an explorer who was severely injured both in body and mind upon his return. He will require a stay in the appropriate hospital to heal and recuperate before he can continue his exploratory travels.

The next stage would be for the Spirit-Soul to face the karmic board. It is NOT a judgement session, but an evaluation, a type of processing of information. It is impossible and illogical to belief that God, who is the ultimate Source of love and light, would deal with such dark and heavy energies as punishments and judgements. Darkness cannot exist where light blazes its radiance, for darkness is but the absence of light.

The board will be chaired by the Spirit-Soul-Self. Supported by its other Soul-partners, the Soul begins to examine the human life it just departed from. Only the negative, heavier part of the Akash will be revealed for the Soul to examine. The Soul is encouraged to put on the hat of the subject, evaluator, examiner and healer, at the same time. The Karmic Board's role is that of counselor, supporter, adjuster and observer in this process. Together they will decide where the Spirit-Soul wishes to go. Some karmic debts can be *paid* within the Earth's Spirit realms if the Soul chooses to remain there. With counseling and the return of awareness of the Soul-Self, the Soul determines how and when it will deal with its karmic ledger. If the Soul decides to reincarnate without the required rest period, it will return with a large backpack of dark energies that have not been transformed and healed. It will script a very challenging life for itself in the hope that it can transmute and pay off a major portion of the debt load.

When a Soul decides to reincarnate, there are many preparations to make and it activates a big planning session. First, the Soul has to find and choose the parents that will assist in providing the environment to pay off this debt load. It has to justify its decision to return, and many can reject its request to play this supporting role. If the Soul cannot find, or reach an agreement with another one at its level of vibration, it becomes a default action. Its supporting Soul-team begins to look for other willing actors at lower vibrational levels.

Parental roles are therefore, a sacred gift to each child. It is painful for any Soul to play the part that requires abuse, anger or rejection. The supporting role is played based on Divine Love of the Soul. This is one reason we are often encouraged to thank our parents without judgement. For in truth, we thank their Soul components for the difficult roles they had to play to help us complete our human life-lessons. The phrase, learning your *life-lessons,* is a human line, for truly the Soul does not need to *learn* anything. For the Soul it is a dream-adventure of discovery. It is the opportunity to experience the awakening within the confinement of human biology known as the rise and expansion of Consciousness from density. This transition can only be achieved through the alchemy of transmutation of dark emotions into light filaments of awareness, knowledge and wisdom.

As the wheel of time continues its rotation upon the Earth plane, so does the Karmic Board continue to monitor and counsel generation after generation of human-soul partnerships. The records of each life, recorded as *a past-life experience* are meticulously kept and any wisdom harvested, shared and made available to all participants. When needed, a specific past life memory would be allowed to enter the human mind in order to provide guidance for the present life. These can usually be obtained through hypnosis, or shamanic rituals. Instigating a past-life regression just for the sake of curiosity will only feed the Ego-mind and does not serve nor assist in the journey of evolution.

Slowly a pattern emerges. Catastrophes, calamities and devastations of massive scales seem to generate a huge surge of compassion and good will among men. Such surges of positive light energies boosted the Karmic Wheel, and big adjustments are made to the Akash as a result of these shifts in the mass emotional field. These periodic natural disasters were agreed to, and implemented, throughout human history to accommodate and maintain the balance of the energetic scale of Consciousness. As a by-product of these episodes, a large number of Souls would vacate the human plane and provide a big opening for the re-incarnation of other Souls who could enhance and speed up the rise to awareness.

After Lemuria, a better prototype of the human vessel needed to be reconfigured, and based on the information gathered, the next model named the Adam Kadmon body type came off the drawing board. The Lemurian experiences were added and wired into higher DNA strands that were kept dormant until the Soul-human would remember and initiate the access codes. It was hoped that this new prototype would be able to process the karmic challenges of future generations more efficiently. The Atlanteans were the embodiment of the early stages of this prototype, and this new structure enabled them to submerge themselves within the deeper emotional layers of biology. The karmic ledgers were very light at first, until the deluge of spiritual debts of Atlantis overshadowed and overwhelmed the board. This heavy load was one of the nodes that caused the imbalance during the times of Atlantis when the level of Consciousness took a rapid and deep dive into the tar pit of dark emotions.

As the result of the decision to re-enter the Earth realms with new tools, the major group karmic debt that had been accumulated during the time of Atlantis were put on hold. It would remain dormant until the time was considered favourable for renewed growth in Consciousness. Small debts were periodically released to be paid according to the level of individual Consciousness and abilities of the subsequent tribal lives on Earth.

CHAPTER FOUR

The Journey of the Warrior

Once the agreement was made to allow the male energies to take the upper hand, the Souls dove deeply and submerged themselves into the heavy role of the Warrior. Within the higher realms of reality, there is no separation of male or female entities. This separation is part of the reality within Duality where opposing forces are the norm. Thus, each Soul must choose which costume to wear upon each reincarnation. As the Age of the Warrior began, those who chose to reincarnate in male bodies learned what it was like to be responsible for the survival of the tribe and to become the warriors whose role was to fight for and protect their families. However, we need to add that, although the warrior energy takes a more dominant role within the males, it is present in the female bodies as well.

The Stone-Age came and went, followed by the Bronze Age, which eventually flowed into the industrial revolution centered on the European continent. Experiencing these ages gave the Soul a different level of awareness and a better understanding of the life cycle of the human body. Human lifespan had been lengthened or shortened on a sliding scale depending on the circumstances of the developing tribes. Longer lifespans were to allow the Soul more opportunities of fully immersing itself in the history of humankind and collecting more wisdom to be recorded and stored in the Akashic Records. For example, one of the longer lifespan periods happened during the time of Abraham where people lived beyond one hundred years. Shorter lives were implemented to provide a faster re-entry for the Souls to speed up the Karmic Wheel during the era of tribal wars, revolutions and the dark ages of the world wars.

Within this compulsion, the human-male-Souls learned to shoulder the heavier roles of responsibility, of being the head of a family and of defending ones country, or belief system. The role of the human male eventually evolved into an illusion that being a male was stronger and better. The warrior male-ego grew within this illusionary platform and created a deeper separation of roles between males and females. In a majority of the societies on Earth, male children were preferred as the future warriors, the future soldiers, and the only ones assumed capable of looking after the family unit.

The male physical body was looked upon as having superior strength, and in some regions, considered to have higher intellect as well. Governments rose as countries declared themselves as independent nations. Males would be elected to form the governing establishments. Boundaries were erected, and the illusion of separation gained strength upon the face of the Earth. The female energies experienced suffering in bondage, subservience, obedience and began to lose sight of the Self. They were often considered non-human and not allowed to have a voice within the community. In many areas they could not show their faces outside the walls of their homes and often would not be allowed to leave their residences.

Intermittently the promise of assistance was sent in the form of more experienced Souls such as Abraham and Moses. These veteran Souls brought the wisdom that they had gained and the memory of Oneness they had retained. Clues were transmitted through them in the form of messages, or teachings such as the Ten Commandments, the Torah and many other sacred scripts to help the Souls navigate their choices.

The Soul group, who became known as the Jews, agreed to become the Chosen People of the world. They were to immerse themselves into the heaviest and darkest goo of the warrior acts of violence and suffering. With the help of the infusion of the teachings and strong faith of Abraham, Moses, and later Jesus, it was hoped that they would be able to purify, and refine this dark energy into the embryos of forgiveness, compassion and love for mankind. The largest shift began with their bondage in Egypt and continued for several generations as they traveled in the dessert for forty years. The desert was thought to be the perfect environment to ignite the strength within the future generation of Jews to face the next layers of darkness. The Holocaust along with the continual persecution of the Chosen People was the energetic strands that dealt with many of the anchoring issues, such as fear, survival, abandonment and the lack of love. They were the initial ones who chose to shoulder the responsibility of stepping into the deeper mines of suffering for everyone. Eventually, there would be other Soul groups who would take up the baton as more and more of the teams descended further into the depths of what some have termed the *tar-pit* of human suffering.

Messages were sent through angelic visitations on a regular basis to the advanced Souls whose assignment was to teach and educate the masses. One of the most prominent Souls was the one known as Jesus. Jesus was born at the beginning of the last two millennia that heralded the final stages of the study of Consciousness. The Mayan Calendar reported it as the end of a twenty-six thousand year cosmic season, and it coincided with the Christian calendar that was based on the birth of the Christ. The new teachings and messages that Jesus presented were eventually transcribed and preserved in the Bible. Its profound message created the hoped for shift in Consciousness, and Christianity spread across the world. Many shamans, prophets and astrologers had already noted the potential direction of the human journey and sent out their discoveries as a warning into the world at large. The end of the year two thousand was the time for the final evaluation of the rise of Human Consciousness. The legend of the horrific method of death that Jesus went through was a humongous episode that would be stamped forever within the Mass Consciousness Mind. Jesus embodied the Christ-Over-Soul Energy and accepted the key components of the dark energies of violence, torture and suffering. With the special tools recognized as the power of Divine Love, he was able to transform this massive dark batch into purified light energy. We could say that he carried the cross of suffering for all of us, for with this very visual act, he started the momentum of the possibility of potential mass enlightenment.

To meet the needs of other areas that have evolved with different customs, traditions and belief systems, other advanced Souls took on the human mantle as well, and walked the earth spreading their messages. Ascended Masters, such as Mohammed, who established the Islamic Faith; Siddhartha Gautama, who became known as the Buddha; and many Indian Gods and Goddesses descended to infuse the Human Mass Mind with the seeds of Divine Love.

It was not an easy process, and there were many times when the dark veils seemed to become heavier and thicker in certain areas. The dark ages in Europe spawned the painful wounds of the Spanish inquisition, and the revolutions in France gave the illusion that things were not moving at all. Human life-spans were shortened for centuries within this era to give the Souls a period of rest and re-evaluation of the life lessons that were chosen. A shorter life provided an opportunity for a quicker return in order to accelerate the process of the alchemy of transformation. It also helped to gain a deeper understanding of the consequences of Karmic debt. The Black Plague was one avenue that provided the door for many Souls to return to the human-Spirit world, opening a big gap for other Souls to enter. It brought in the beginning of awareness of what was needed to maintain a better and healthier human life style, in that era of ignorance towards sanitation.

The industrial revolution swept across Europe and changed the structure of that civilization, once again. Different religions took hold and grew, spreading their faith across the face of the world. The warrior energy grew in strength within the male reincarnates, as they continue to plunge into dissention within the family unit that grew into tribal wars and eventually into civil wars across the globe.

The ability to navigate the oceans became a reality and new lands were discovered. The societies in Europe saw themselves as the civilized world, and the warriors turned into conquerors and used their more advanced weapons to conquer and claim other lands. The European navigators roamed the oceans in search of new colonies to enrich themselves. They flooded the Americas, and new countries were born. The new occupants not only brought their religious beliefs and customs, but they also unleashed the dark river of oppression over the native populace and sowed the abomination of slavery.

It seemed as if the warrior energies held the reins of violence and continued to grow in strength as it marched into the quagmire of disrespect for human life. Massacres and the addiction of power over others permeated every corner of the so called civilized society. The slide into the dark pit during the Altlantean ages seemed to be happening all over again. This time it occurred on all the major continents. At one point, it seemed as if the level of Consciousness was barely moving. There was sluggishness in its growth and something needed to jar it into action.

It came in the form of the escalation of civil wars, wherein numerous countries began to demand a release from domination by others. Awareness of injustice and human rights slowly infiltrated the human Consciousness. Throughout the ages of men, many advanced Souls were at times choosing to re-enter to assist a shift and embody the tools that would unlock the hidden files within the human mind. One such was

Abraham Lincoln, who turned the tide against slavery in North America, and much later there was Mahatma Ghandi, who brought emancipation for India through non-violent means. In the twentieth century there was Nelson Mandela, who saw the human-Soul journey with clarity and encouraged awareness through his own personal life experiences.

The warrior mindset, however, was not completely satisfied and escalated their demands for world domination and control. It was the match that ignited the World Wars. Again the ancient lands in Europe became ground zero, the nursery where these horrific wars were germinated. The First World War was apparently not enough to cause a great shift in Consciousness and was soon followed by the Second World War.

The Soul who came as Hitler was needed to ignite the fuse for an intense transformational era in world history. He was the great stick that was plunged into the tar-pit, churning and spinning the darkness to the surface. His propaganda of superiority and self-righteousness was brought to everyone's attention with his attacks on the neighboring lands. Soon, the horror could not be denied any longer by the world community. His dark agenda swept across Europe, shattering any chance of peace. His occupation was a black boiling shadow of intense fear, hopelessness, despair, and included the desperate pains of hunger.

Once again, the Jews, the Chosen People played a major role in this purging. As a Soul-group they agreed to become the sacrificial lambs and to experience the hateful and horrific acts of persecution via the Holocaust. As a Soul-group they shouldered *the next Cross of Suffering* for humanity. Their sacrifice ignited sparks of compassion, courage and heroism within many hearts. It fanned the flames of indignation and protests and awakened the awareness of the dark presence of horror. It opened the eyes of the world community to the realization that humans are capable of unthinkable atrocities. The counter cries of unacceptability of such barbarous, inhumane acts gave rise to heroism. Soldiers bravely gave their lives for their fellow men, resulting in a raising of the level of Mass Consciousness. Many put their lives on the line to hide and save others from unjustified imprisonment and torture. Still others within the occupied lands bravely formed the Underground Resistance groups, which courageously assisted the rescue efforts of the liberating forces.

The United States of America was forced to enter the fray reluctantly through the attack on Pearl Harbour. This cleansing, violent war raged within the four directions, from West to East and to North and South. It was a major, intense confrontation of the two forces of Duality.

The world shook and took a deep cleansing breath as the devastating mushroom cloud of the atomic bombs drifted slowly across the Japanese skies. It was an intense fire of purification that blazed across the dark night of suffering.

The war experience eventually began to soften the male warrior mind as it came to realize the futility and the illogical acts of the killing spree of war. For the female heart, it became an intolerable pain of grief through the experience of losing loved ones. The deluge of tears was the sacred rain that washed away the ashes from the fires of war and began to clear the heavy emotional thunderstorms across the globe. The combined cry of *"No more"* from many voices exploded into the heavens and gave rise to a tsunami of compassion that roared across the earth's mantle. This awareness initiated the awakening within the female incarnates as they began to look at their roles in a different way. The men were all enlisted for the war and had to leave their families and their homes. This forced the women to shoulder the responsibilities of survival for the families left behind. Suddenly, the women took on different roles that they never thought they could ever occupy. They embraced their new capabilities and their self-worth, self-esteem and self-realization took a huge leap forward. It nudged the Divine Feminine Consciousness to stir and to turn its slumbering gaze towards the long awaited potentiality of mass awakening.

The purging of the Second World War affected every country on Earth, directly or indirectly. There was excitement among the Soul groups as the possibility of a potential greater Shift in Consciousness could be sensed on the horizon. Numerous vacancies were opened after the war, once more providing entry for many Souls. This was the long awaited time for the old Altantean Souls who were promised a return for another chance to experience the awakening of the Soul-Spirit in human form. For the next half century, these old Souls reincarnated and took their place in society. At the same time, in preparation for this great potential, many Souls agreed to become additional hosts as human Aspects for the Ascended Masters, Archangels and other Light-Beings who are part of the Earth Adventure. For most of the aspects these attributes were kept hidden until such time that the potential would reveal itself.

Upon further assessment, it was determined that there was still a great imbalance between the male and female energies. Even though the warrior stream was slowly losing steam, it was still very strong in many areas, and in some corners of the world, it was deeply rooted in tradition, customs and belief systems. The Divine Feminine had not fully awakened within the hearts and minds of the female human hosts, even though the roles of women in the western worlds have taken a drastic change.

It was also noted that the imbalance was greatly affected by the energy of the human Ego. The accepted definition of Ego, as depicted in the dictionary, is *that part of the mind which has a sense of individuality and the superego related to self-esteem, self-centeredness and conceit*. The Ego was part of the wiring system when the human construct was created and could never be separated from the human structure. Trying to eliminate it would be similar to dismembering one of the wires within the main frame of your computer. It is, therefore, a vital part of the Soul-human anchoring system and cannot be denied or ignored. Without it, the Soul portion of this combination would, and could not be fully anchored in the density of the Third Dimension. The Ego kept the Soul from remembering its true nature and its connection to the Source of Divine Light. It was part of the blindfold, and it is the component, the glue, that keeps the human-Soul anchored in Duality. Its role is to constantly persuade the human mind that it knows all the answers. It encourages judgements and criticisms and frequently presents delectable dark temptations on a platter. The Ego-desire body becomes a robe of glory that dominates and directs the human personality. To keep control over human lives, the Ego created many departments, each functioning under the Ego's mandate. **FEAR** is the comptroller that overshadows all the other areas, and when allowed full rein, it will constantly influence every decision a human makes.

Through fear, the Ego tries to confuse the mind with its persuasive whispers. It makes the mind think that putting the Self down, having low self-esteem, wrapping oneself with self-righteousness and unrealistic humility, are not egoistic behaviours. It is a very strong illusion, for it is the negative side of the Ego and its influence can be just as destructive as the positive side, where one considers oneself to be of superior standing. The two faces of the Ego found a very strong foothold in the warrior energy and flourished within the lower layers of Consciousness.

Linear time moved along its track, and the Industrial Age moved into the Age of Commercialism after the Second World War. At first, there was hope that the peace agreement between the major world powers would provide an opportunity for the warrior energy to mellow and begin to acknowledge the presence of its partner, the gentle feminine energies. Instead, it chose to rebuild its powerhouse and entered another road to travel.

There were high hopes when the sacred words of light, "*In God we trust*," were anchored in the document of the constitution of the United States of America. This new country that was born out of the ashes of the European generation of warriors was given a new start and a new slate upon which to build a great nation. It became a receptacle for members of the world tribes to plant new roots for a new generation of a united brotherhood. It grew into the center of the potentiality of possibilities so that the awakening and the transformation of the Souls could begin within this country. However, as time went by, it looked as if this hoped for Unity-Awareness did not manifest, instead it created more separation within the Mass-Mind.

For the next centuries, it seemed as if the warrior transferred its focus into building a huge commercial empire, and the energies of war shifted into a subtly hidden agenda of deceit and aggression for the sake of profit. A different war has descended upon the world's societies, a war of avariciousness. The guidelines of the Ten Commandments were either ignored, thrown into dusty drawers, or its message distorted and misinterpreted. The monitoring council decided to interfere and began to send its messengers to offer more positive alternatives for the human-Souls to choose from.

The Divine Feminine Energy stirred, and agreed to initiate a series of apparitions, of visual appearances of the Holy Mother Mary, as its channel. Mary was, and is a well-known and loved representative of the Divine Mother. She was the perfect messenger. She gave many messages through different channels all over the world, in an attempt to infuse the warrior stream with the nurturing love strands of compassion and love of brotherhood/sisterhood within humanity. Mary became the focus of the Mass Feminine Mind through world-wide prayers, and it slowly began to strengthen the Feminine energies, in an attempt towards balance.

A wave of anticipation rolled across the Universe as the world rumbled into the decades of the last two thousand year linear time slot, allotted the human-Soul quest.

PART TWO
The Great Shift

CHAPTER ONE

The Eleventh Hour

Two-thousand years ago, a special Soul volunteered to enter the Earth Realms to be used as an extraordinary tool to jar the memory of the Christ-seed within the heart into Human-Mass-Consciousness. A special human vessel was needed to provide a host for the Christ Soul, and the story of Christmas was born. Because of the dominant male energies, Jesus had to come in as a male in order to make himself heard. In order to maintain balance, his feminine counterparts were Mary, his Mother and anchor, and Mary Magdalene, a quiet partner who would walk with him. Jesus was the huge rock that was thrown into the pond of Consciousness and was expected to cause a two thousand year rippling effect across the world. By accepting the cup of mass suffering, and shouldering the burden of the cross for all of us, he laid down the first stones for the foundation of the path to enlightenment. The cross was the symbol of the imbalance of the male/female energies within Duality. When asked the question of where the path led to, Jesus stated, *"I am the Path"*.

Many belief systems interpreted his sacrifice as an act of taking on all our sins so that we may be forgiven by God, the Creator. It took humanity two thousand years to reach the understanding, and the awareness that *sin* was a creation of the Ego-self, for it promoted the heavy baggage of *guilt and low self-esteem*. The word *forgiveness* does not, and cannot exist in the vocabulary of Pure Light, for in the eyes of Source, the Ultimate Creator God, there was nothing to forgive. The notion of wrongness that needed forgiveness and absolution was part of the Duality environment, and it is therefore impossible for that energy to exist in the realm of Divine Love. Every *evil* act perpetrated by the human was a valuable experience for the Soul. It was an opportunity to refine and purify the dark deed into a filament of higher vibrations using the energy of words of light, such as forgiveness, as a conduit for transformation.

Two thousand years ago, the Earth was still mired in a heavy, low warrior frequency, and it took Jesus, the Christ-Soul, forty days isolated in the harsh desert to *face the devil,* who was none other than his human-Ego-self. To show us the way, Jesus had to walk every step of the Path as a human-Soul being as well. His strong Soul component was able to master the Ego temptations and transform it into the power that would enable him to face the energies of abandonment, betrayal, humiliation and torture. He acknowledged the human bondage by voicing the weight of abandonment with the words, *"Father why have you forsaken me?"* He then initiated the transformation with the crucial bridging words of forgiveness," *Forgive them for they know not what they do."* The Crucifixion and the legend of the Resurrection created a major shift in the fabric of Duality. As the apostles spread the words of Love, Christianity took root in many parts of the world. It took many years, but it spread, consuming the Roman Empire and eventually gaining acceptance throughout Europe. Unfortunately the message of Unconditional Divine Love became distorted and polluted by the Duality-Ego-Mind as the centuries went by and the core of the true message was lost in the re-telling and the subsequent teachings.

In order to meet the requirements of *Free Will,* other Master Souls, such as Mohammed and the Buddha, entered the Earth Realms to provide the religious diversity and choices for every human-Soul in every corner of the world. Every message transmitted, broadcasted and taught by these Masters and Gurus, carry the same message, based on Unconditional Love. Each must discern the truth from the messages, as written and formalized by men, while honoring other belief systems. The final challenge is to ferret out the truth within their own faction, and then join each unique section to form the great tapestry of the whole truth of Creation. Imagine each belief to be a piece of a puzzle. Each piece has a vital part of the truth, and each has its unique spot to complete the whole picture. With one single piece missing, the new picture cannot be completed.

With Free-Will, the belief systems took a life of their own, over the passage of time. The main message of Love became distorted and perverted and hidden behind the lies and the murmurs of

the Control-Ego-self. It created a big challenge for the seeker of enlightenment. Many Souls became lost again, as they allowed themselves to be persuaded to swim in the tar-pit of human indulgences and atrocities. In this environment of Duality, society was instilled with the belief that the illusions bombarded by the mainstream media were the way life was supposed to be. Within the last two centuries, materialism and commercialism dominated every walk of life in the civilized world. Material abundance became the desired goal of the populace, and lack of it was met with despair, hopelessness and the illusion of lack of respect in society.

The monitoring Soul-council kept their vigil, for amidst the darkness they could still detect some bright sparks of light diligently held by committed spiritual Seekers. This was considered strong evidence that all was not lost and there was still hope for a successful outcome. A sense of the possibility of the long awaited potentiality shimmered within the fabric of Creation. There was restlessness within the Unity Consciousness, the God Consciousness of All That Is, and a feeling of excited anticipation. It had faith in its children and waited for the potentiality to open its doors. In the eyes of the Great Creator, success of the endeavor was already on its way.

The new ingredient, the raw material of new energies, had been found, mined and examined. The question, however, was whether each symbiotic Soul-human construct could turn itself into a transformer, a laboratory of alchemy, and refine the strands of dark emotion into finer strands of higher love frequency. Could the Soul-human gather all the members of its internal orchestra, and begin to tune all the instruments within that it may burst forth into perfect harmony of its own unique musical score? Could each choose to discover and access the hidden seed of light, the drop of Divine Love, and the essence of the Unified Field of Creation within the heart chamber? Within this inter-dimensional sacred space lies the Christ Seed of light, the key that will open the gate leading to the first step on the pathway to enter evolution and transformation of the human-Soul partnership. The Divine Love energy is the glue, the unifier and the component that will allow the Soul-human to transcend and move beyond the walls of Duality.

The specification of the Soul-contract was that all Souls involved in this journey must evolve as one unit to reach the level of consciousness necessary to break through the dimensional barrier. It was taken into consideration that not all will be able to reach the new levels at the same time, and provisions were put in place to accommodate different time lines of awakening. No one will be ignored, no Soul will be without assistance, and no one will be left behind. No matter how long it takes in linear Earth time.

As the twentieth century marched in, it generated a mixture of starts and stops. The rebuilding of many nations after the Second World War brought hope and a sigh of relief within the hearts of men. The emotional and mental state of the Mass-Mind when world peace was declared, allowed the Mass Consciousness to step-up onto the next level. This was a long awaited signal for the old Atlantean Souls. They claimed the promise to return and many reincarnated during this time period to complete and fulfill their destiny. They are the first wave of spiritual teachers who will be awakened to their full potential at the onset of the Great Shift.

As the world settled into a rebuilding mode after the war, it witness the birth of the movement of the flower-children, the so-called Hippies. It quickly spread over North America. It created hope that the understanding of the true meaning of Divine Love might enter the infant Consciousness of mankind. It did initiate a slight shift, but not enough momentum to push the human train of Consciousness into a higher track. This attempt at pushing the Mass-Mind into a more loving frequency was unfortunately tempered by the naive ignorance of the Flower-children. They were persuaded and believed in the illusion that the euphoria reached by drug use was the way to enter a spiritual, alternate, enlightened state. Instead they exposed themselves to a drug induced chemical imbalance in the brain wave patterns that created the illusion of an alternate state. It gave them a false impression, a delusion of well-being and a distorted view of the love-energy they were seeking.

The monitoring teams increased their vigilance as the year 2000 crept closer and closer. The messages of Armageddon were coming to the surface creating a wave of fear and anxiety around the globe. Many groups were suddenly interested in the ancient texts searching for more positive messages to alleviate their fears. The predictions in Revelations in the Bible became popular reading material. Messages of Seers such as Edgar Cayce and Nostradamus were brought to the world's attention once more and instigated active debates within various spiritual communities.

Unknown to the human awareness however, things were already in place to terminate the whole experiment if the rise of Consciousness did not meet the agreed upon levels. The engineering team had prepared a more devastating scenario than the one they had programmed for Atlantis. A massive asteroid hidden behind one of the planets in this galaxy was programmed to hurdle itself towards Earth the moment the destruct button was activated. A magnetic target deep into the Earth's crust was already in place as a bull's-eye homing device in the North American continent to begin the elimination process. The plan was for all Souls to vacate and for all life forms to evacuate out of the Three-Dimensional-Earth plane, because it was originally created as a temporary place for the Souls' investigative journey into Duality.

The year 1987 was a year wherein a full polling of all sentient beings was held. With bated breath the monitoring council watched as the level of mass consciousness slowly rose. With a shout of joy, all watched as a small group of Soul-light-drops emerged from a dark corner of the world and tipped the scale, triggering the Harmonic Convergence that catapulted the world into the Great Shift. The thirteen remaining years until the year 2000 were but a blink of an eye for the council, however, for the human journey it was the eleventh hour. The year 2000 was the measuring bar, and with the removal of this bar, it became the starting line for a planet-wide construction site.

With a sigh of relief the self-destruct command was immediately aborted, and an excited flurry of activity erupted within all the stations at every dimensional level. For the next few years NASA, the space agency noticed an increase in space debris, such as asteroid chunks that somehow bypassed the Earth.

There were only thirteen Earth-years left to complete all the preparations for the new project. All the angelic teams that were on a standby mode were alerted and commissioned into action. They all realized that everything, every component, had to be changed, restructured, recalibrated and some parts completely remodeled and rebuilt, before the move into a higher dimensional harbor could happen. These changes not only apply to the Earth, but also to every occupant, especially the humans. The Goddess repeatedly emphasized the message that EVERYTHING has to be changed, recalibrated, and rebuilt. I did not grasp the complete meaning of her message at first until much later in my own journey.

It was time for the Soul-drops to return home but not to their old home. They could not return to their former residence. As anticipated, they had changed beyond measure and had earned the first right to move to a brand new location. It would be a very special home, a second creation that had yet to be built with all the Souls' input on a new transformed Earth. The Souls had fallen in love with the beauty of nature on the Earth, and as they transcended into a new frequency, so will the Earth. Gaia, the great entity, who had guarded the Earth and its occupants for eons of time, has completed her assignment and wants to go home to her own dimensional reality. She is leaving the Earth as an inheritance for the occupants of the New Earth. In other words, we, the new occupants, will be the next guardians of an interdimensional Earth reality and take on the mantle of the new Earth-Mothers and Fathers. Again, we repeat that the higher frequencies of consciousness cannot exist in the lower third dimension. It can only exist in the fifth dimension where the higher vibration of Love-Light resides.

Within this new space, a structure would be created using building blocks that contain the combined, accumulated wisdom and experiences of the Souls' human journey. This was a massive undertaking, and many teams had to be coordinated to get things started. Preliminary steps had to be implemented to prepare for the great Shift, and it immediately began with the arrival of the electromagnetic angelic team under the leadership of the archangel Kryon. This team had to recalibrate the electromagnetic grid that was created as a protective and an anchoring shield around the Earth. The magnetic poles of the earth also had to be shifted, and this of course would affect the angle of the Earth's axis and eventually, the Earth's rotation. This little blue planet had to lift its anchor from its three-dimensional harbor and prepare for an extraordinary voyage through inter-dimensional gates to a new parking spot in a fifth dimensional reality of existence. In order to make this possible, every etheric layer within the Earth realms had to go through a dismantling and a recalibration process, including the non-physical Earth-spirit realms and the physical electromagnetic stratospheric and atmospheric layers.

The Earth reacted to the new codes and began to readjust its structure. Weather patterns changed as the trend of global warming became a new concept for the anxious minds of men. Many began to point their fingers at mass pollution caused by the world-wide industrialization. The human Ego-self thinks that global warming is all caused by human industries without considering Gaia's influence. They do not understand, nor can many humans accept the fact, that Gaia, the Earth-Mother, is a very powerful entity and has the ability to cleanse herself if she so wishes. However the choice to proceed with the act of

KYRON

Global warming

↑ been saying for years.

harming the Earth with pollution was part of the human life lessons. Even with visual evidence appearing everywhere, some still refused to take steps to control pollution and heal the Earth. It was a section of Duality that challenged the Mass Mind to make a choice between a polluted world controlled by materialistic industrialisation, or a clean Earth with a reduced profit margin. Mahatma Gandhi summed it in a profound way, *"The earth provides enough to satisfy man's need, but not every man's greed."*

Global warming is a necessary process and Gaia allowed it in preparation for the potential shift to occur. With the advent of global warming, she began to initiate the required steps to facilitate the restructuring. Heat is created when friction is increased between two opposing forces and the Earth is in the process of revving up its internal engines in preparation for the big move. Every particle is retuned to resonate with the higher frequencies, and when this mandate was implemented, the four Earth elements responded. Like the motor in an engine, everything has to spin faster to increase momentum. Atoms spin and move very slowly in dense matter but spin with a faster speed in lighter materials. For example, ice particles are thick and dense but when heated turns into water. When heated again, it transforms into steam, fog or mists that soon become invisible in the fast spinning molecules of air. Imagine that we are the ice droplets that have to change into finer mist particles, for our new world is not only the air but the ethers, the faster and higher frequencies of the fifth element.

Imagine having to restructure a spaceship that requires the capability of travelling past the moon, and the Milky Way into another distant unknown galaxy within a different universe. Not only does the ship need to be redesigned and restructured but all the passengers that would be travelling in the ship would have to go through a similar overhaul. The Earth is the spaceship that will carry us on this tremendous voyage that has never been attempted before in the history of creation. It will truly be a maiden voyage of exploration and discovery, a journey *"where no Soul has gone before."*

At this juncture, the Goddess returned to the Mini-Miner analogy to enhance clarity of the concept of this momentous time of change. The project of the Mini-Miners had a time line, and the end of this last rotation was approaching. The monitoring teams were getting worried at this point. The Miners were not processing the raw crude oil as fast as expected. Every time they refined a section, the products were collected in specific containers, examined and evaluated by the monitoring groups.

The initial contract called for a certain quantity of the final product to be mined and produced to meet the quota needed to justify the expense of opening this special mining operation. A self-destruct signal was coded into the main computer in the control room to close the mine shaft forever if the contract could not be met.

The dead line was close at hand, and it was time to proceed with the final weighing of the product which had been amassed. Nervously the team-members gathered in the control room outside the entrance cave and watched the dial slowly rise and hover just below the lowest acceptable target line. There was an intense pause as everyone stared at the dial. Anxious questions rushed through their minds: "Was this the end? Were they to be eliminated? Was the project about to be discarded? Would everyone lose their jobs? What would happen to the Mini-Miners?"

Suddenly at the eleventh hour, tiny footsteps hurried into the storage room and a very tired, scruffy looking miner rushed in carrying a small vat of clear, refined oil. He climbed onto the platform above the main container and began to pour the golden liquid into the container. With bated breath, all eyes were riveted to the dial. Suddenly, a shout of triumph and joy erupted as the arrow on the dial crept and then stabilized on the designated mark. The scientific researchers congratulated each other enthusiastically, thumped each other's back and danced in celebration. There was a sigh of relief when the chief engineer quickly turned off the self-destruct button.

A new directive was put into action, and immediately the appropriate machines began to hum as huge belts on multiple engines shuddered into a faster rotation. The mechanisms of ignition coils began to use the refined fuel to generate an intense beam of light that lit up the whole shaft with a brilliant powerful flash. They could finally see the richness of the mine's vein and the great, unlimited potential it could generate for generations and generations of creativities. The beam grew in intensity as it fed upon this different refined fuel. To everyone's amazement, it revealed not only all the hidden corners of the shaft, but the light particles that had evolved and morphed into many unique, unusual qualities affecting everything it touched.

At first, the miners rejoiced that their assignment was over and that they could go home at last. But when the great light allowed them to see with clarity the home that they had occupied for so long, they realized that they could not, and did not want to go back, to their old home. Somehow they had fallen in love with the land and their way of life. They had lived in this containment field for generations and had accumulated history of their experiences. Everyone involved was aware of the risks involved. A prolonged exposure to the environment of the mine could have an irreversible change in the DNA component of the miners. Together they made a collective choice to stay as they were. No one, however, anticipated what could and would happen when the intense light particles of the beams bathed the miners and swept across the narrow, rough mine walls.

The DNA strands within the miners had adjusted to the environment during their sojourn in the pit and its essence had merged with the particles of the mine itself. The beam began to pulse with multi colored waves of light and emitted strange harmonious sound frequencies that started a series of unprecedented transformations. This new combined energy flowed and swirled over the occupants and the surrounding structures. At that very moment the miners knew instinctively that they had to release everything they had ever known, detach from all attachments, and surrender to the light completely to allow the metamorphoses to occur.

The stunned observers saw the mutated gene within the miners beginning to morph resulting in an astonishing rapid growth spurt. As the miners began to transform into larger beings, the mine itself responded at the same time and began to enlarge, expanding the shaft. The walls trembled, rumbled, collapsed, then exploded outward, and the narrow shaft was no more. The old mine was dismantled as it imploded upon itself. What rose out of the debris was a mind-boggling surprise to everyone. The whole area transformed into a valley whose surrounding area was comprised of hills upon fertile hills of the pulsing refined, rich, purified veins of the mine. It was a miraculous magical moment for all participants.

In response to the combined wishes of the collective mind of the mining society, a new home came into existence. The excited observers, who were strategically stationed outside the epicenter of the quake, frantically readjusted their equipment and recorded the momentous occasion. All the ledges had disappeared with the explosion, and through the dusty veils of debris, the witnesses noticed a miraculous sight. All the members of the supporting teams stationed on the ledges were slowly drifting down and being pulled along the silver cord until they merged with the changed miners. This was immediately followed by the amazing action of the main parent of each miner who had been waiting at the entrance of the cave. They followed suit and were drawn along the pulsing, connecting, communication lines, mutating, transforming, and evolving into a new composite whole Being that finally united with the miners in the valley. A fully aware citizen of a new world emerged to populate and start a very different life in a magical valley where all dreams can come true.

CHAPTER TWO

The Lotus Connection

Once again I joined the Goddess on the marble patio facing the limitless pond of the lotus. This exquisite, tranquil and peaceful place touched my heart and moved me deeply every time I entered this reality. It seemed to affect Quan Yin the same way as she gazed fondly towards the pond admiring the beautiful multi-colored lotus blossoms. I recalled that in the ancient tongue her name meant *"Born of the Lotus,"* and I remembered the visions she had sent me as I awakened from the dream of Spirit. In the first dream, I saw a baby being birthed out of a lotus. It was a living, cooing baby, but it was made out of clear, crystalline water. It was a puzzle that I could not fathom for a long time until she gifted me the next vision. In this dream a beautiful naked female figure emerged from the lotus and again she was a vibrant, living sculpture of crystalline water particles. After having gone through the purging of my dark, traumatic, emotional layers, I gained the understanding of the visions and resonated with her profound connection to the life-cycle of the Lotus. On that day I looked forward to the fact that she was about to relate another version of her tale of the Lotus to enhance her narrative of the human journey.

She smiled at me before she began, "Remember who you truly are for you are also born of the Lotus. Now let us embark on a parallel path to our story with another lotus saga."

"Once upon a time there lived an avid gardener in a fertile valley. The gardener had filled his extensive garden with many plants, flowers, vegetables and fruit trees creating a beautiful landscape of scents and colors. One day he decided to create a different kind of garden at the far corner of his land and began to dig a very deep, large hole. He dug and

73

dug through layers of sand, big stones, gravel and clay and discovered, to his delight, that a spring of clear water sprang up from the middle of the hole. The spring giggled, bubbled and danced into the hole, creating a very large pond. The gardener was ecstatic and felt that this was to be a special corner in his garden, potentially a very magical place. He began to implement a design for this watery panorama. He began by creating a border garden as a living frame around the pond by planting tall graceful grass-like specimens such as bulrushes, or cattails followed by colorful Irises and other swamp flowers. Next he introduced fishes, turtles and other water animals to inhabit and play in this new water world. As a final touch, he positioned comfortable benches strategically around the pond."

She continued her narrative of the gardener's life, recounting his daily admiration of his watery creation. However, somehow he felt as if there was something still missing. The pond did not feel complete. He did not quite know what it was and so he embarked on an expedition to discover the missing link. He decided to travel far and wide and visited every garden he could find. Then one day as he walked through a forest, he came upon a breath-taking sight. Before him were a number of interconnecting pools of different sizes and shapes. Each was connected to the other by gently flowing brooks. He fell in love with what he encountered. Everywhere he looked he saw beautiful, flowers of every color and shape gently floating on the glass-like, sparkling watery surface. He discovered that the blooms were called Lotuses and knew instantly that he had found the missing component for his special pond. He began collecting a variety of lotus seeds, some ordinary ones, some rare ones and some very extraordinary ones.

Upon his return he invited all his family and friends for a special gathering and asked them to join him in a planting ceremony. Everyone was pleased to come and on a bright sunny day they joined him around the pond. He gave each a handful of seeds and asked that they bless the seeds with loving words and harmonious songs as they gently dropped the seeds into the water.

The seeds arched through the air and fell with tiny splashes as they broke through the surface of the pond. One particular seed was very curious and observant and instinctively understood that it was entering a special phase in its life-cycle. This is its story.

The seed had a last look around as it too was released into the air. It felt the air brushing against its skin as it gained momentum towards the water. It felt and heard the splash and found itself descending gently into the watery environment. "What an adventure", it thought as it drifted down and down, deeper and deeper into the density of cloudy waters. It was a strange sensation for the seed to feel the heavier pressures of this cloudy environment. Soon it reached more shadowy and murkier levels and wondered why the light seemed to be further and further away. Its trajectory finally deposited it into a thick muddy pocket. It felt the pressure of the water push it deeper into this pocket and it was quickly completely buried, enveloped within a dark cocoon-like space. It was very dark for light was completely absent in this enclosed, muddy environment.

The seed was in shock and shook with fright and loneliness. It could neither see nor sense any other living thing and felt abandoned, isolated and imprisoned. The seed hid in this dark place, too afraid to allow anything to pierce its protective shell. It was so consumed with fear that it forgot who it was, where it came from and why it was there. It slumbered for a time mired in dark and fearful dreams.

With time, the seed's survival instincts jarred it into wakefulness, and it realized it had to make a decision. This dark place was its home now, and it decided to embrace its situation and try to create the best scenario possible for its present life. It began to allow its shell to absorb the nutritious muddy water, and the seed drank gratefully, nourishing itself. It was surprised when it realized that its shell was equipped with a sophisticated filtering system. The liquid that seeped out of its filters was not muddy at all, but was a clear elixir of life. It only contained the minerals and compounds that the seed needed for its survival. With this healthy food source, the seed grew and began to send out roots to absorb more sustenance. The roots were tube-like with pipe-like filtration systems that continued to purify what the seed needed from the mud. When dissected, a lotus root looks like a circular wheel where the thick membranes of the spokes are the walls of the channels through which the muddy water is filtered and purified. It is a marvelous process of alchemy that was built into the seed's molecular structure.

After a while, the seed was feeling much better and began to explore its new home. It had an adventurous nature and decided that being frightened was not beneficial to its growth. It discovered that since the roots had such a capable filtering system it could get more food by sending bigger and longer roots deeper into the mud. It was darker further down and the roots had to push through rocks and other obstacles but the results were very favourable. The food extracted from these deeper layers allowed the seed the opportunity to grow faster and stronger. It provided the strength to break through its barrier shell birthing an infant seedling with a tender growing tip. The birth of the infant shoot activated an instinctive compulsion to grow upwards and to seek something it did not quite understand. It had no memory of its former life but knew that it was to embark on another exciting voyage through new and different pathways.

The seed's growing tip was like a *seeing-eye* and it observed its environment with wonder and a desire for knowledge. The tip felt that there was something else out there as it bravely faced the journey that was full of challenges and hazards. The seed realized that it was vital that its roots were firmly grounded in the muddy and rocky layers deep below to ensure a safe anchor before its journey. Without this secure harbor, the seedling knew that it could be wrenched away floating helplessly, getting lost forever in the wide beyond. It could already feel the oppressive, gravitational tug of the mud and the strong pull of the water currents.

With all preparations ready, the young shoot began its voyage upwards, growing into a tender stalk that learned to sway with the current instead of fighting against its forces. As it ventured through the shadowy murky depths, it encountered strange and interesting objects. There were other living creatures that shared this space. Different fishes were swimming and bumping into the young stalk, trying to nibble at it and other water plants whipped and lashed against its tender skin. The stalk swayed and danced away, using the channels of the water currents to avoid all the dangers. It was able to stay on its upward course, for it was supported firmly by its strong roots.

It was about to enter a layer of less density when the stalk saw another of its kind. It immediately turned and was about to greet this neighbor happily, when it noticed something odd about it. This other stalk was not as healthy and strong, as it was only anchored by a single thin root that desperately clung to a clump of rocky mud. It had other roots but these were loosely floating around the stalk in the muddy waters below. This stalk did not have enough nourishment for it had only a thin, shallowly anchored root, and the other floating roots could not get much out of the murky waters they were swimming in either. It was a struggle for this stalk to grow upwards for its weak anchorage could not keep it steady. It was frequently battered by the currents and other inhabitants that kept knocking it off course.

"What happened to you?" shouted the healthy stalk. "I was scared," answered the weak stalk miserably. "That mud felt so strange, and it is so dark down there. I don't want to live in this place. It is not my home. I want to get out of here fast. I needed food, and at first sent out some roots, but I didn't like the muddy flavor and pulled my other roots out. I don't like the feel of that dirty, muddy bottom. I only keep one root down there because I don't like the idea of floating in this dark soup." The healthy stalk felt very sorry for this fellow occupant as it continued to complain about its life. The strong stalk sadly realized that it could not do anything to help the unhappy stalk.

It was about to continue its journey when it saw another stalk. This one was more bizarre for it had no grounding roots at all. The healthy root watched in astonishment as this stalk floated by with all its roots hanging loose around its base. The stalk itself appeared stunted and seemed not to have enough energy to grow. Once more the healthy stalk hailed it: "How are you?" A faint and scattered answer reached the stable stalk. "I am fine, I am not afraid of this silly and stupid place. I am a very special seed and I deserve a better spot. Why should I lower myself into that black mud and feed myself with that dirty food? Why should I allow that darkness to contaminate my pure and lovely self? My splendid roots can and are able to get enough food from the waters around me until I find a better place to live. Besides I am . . . . "The stalk could not hear the rest of the conversation as the emaciated stalk drifted away on the forever moving current. Helplessly, the healthy stalk realized that the chance for this poor, disillusioned stalk to reach the surface was very slim. Until it anchored itself in a safe muddy spot and accepted its new life, it would forever float and drift with the current and remain in the shadowy layers for the rest of its life.

The sturdy stalk moved on through the barriers of the shadowy depths and reached the band of clear waters. It kept its gaze upwards and excitedly noticed the shimmering light high above. It strengthened its resolve to reach that light and asked its roots to increase the clear purified, nutritious liquid to give it a growth spurt. Then one day, conquering its fear of the unknown and with a burst of energy, the stalk breached the surface barrier. It propelled itself from the watery womb and entered a new world. With awe, it looked around this new vista. Everything it had ever known was not there any longer. Nothing looked familiar; everywhere it gazed was foreign to its sight. There were no fish and no watery currents to bar its journey. It faced an unending horizon, a blue sky where things flew in the air and a golden light that shone everywhere. A new life was unfolding before it, and yet, it felt safe for it was still connected to the anchoring roots. It lifted its face and felt the warmth of the sun, and the caressing touch of the wind. Joyfully it knew that it was safely held within the arms of Mother Earth below and that all was well within the Oneness of Creation.

It stepped into this new life with enthusiasm and exuberance resulting in the unfurling of its enormous green leaves. These beautiful green disks gently cradled and stabilized the stalk while the roots far below kept it safely anchored in nourishing mud. It grew into a unique water plant that now fed of the clear waters, fresh air and warming sunlight. The heat of the sun initiated a chemical process within the cells of the leaves creating a different food. It combined the liquid sustenance from the roots with the new intake of air and rain water, creating an alchemy of change that gave it a more powerful elixir. This higher frequency sustenance was so energizing that it gave rise to distant forgotten memories within its cells, and among its leaves, the new plant gave birth to a bud.

Another dawn came, heralding a new day, as the sun rose above the horizon. Radiant golden beams brushed a tender kiss at the bud. The burgeoning, well-fed bud awakened, responded and stretched, and shimmering petals burst forth from its tender cocoon. A new exquisite, pink lotus blossom emerged. Deep within its core, the seed marvelled, for it vaguely remembered that its parent was a red lotus.

Joyfully the blossom lifted its petals towards the warm rays and became aware of its new surroundings. It gazed in wonder at the unending blue sky and the slowly drifting white clouds, as it felt the caressing breeze of the wind. It was astonished to realize that the water around it was as clear as glass and that the whispering ripples formed a comforting cradle. The lotus plant thought that this was a wonderful, magical world and felt very grateful that it had reached this special place. With delightful chuckles, it welcomed the dragonflies, butterflies and other insects to land upon its leaves and petals. It was so enthralled at this new life that it wished to share it with every part of its being. It began to send all its happy thoughts and all the beauty it saw, including the warm, bright rays of the sun, down through its sturdy stalk to the roots far below.

Days passed and the lotus witnessed the surfacing of more and more plants of its kind. Soon the great pond became a show case of brilliant, extra-ordinary lotus flowers in full bloom. The lotus welcomed each emerging blossom joyfully, recognizing each as a family member. These happy, tranquil days of existence seemed to stretch forever for the pink lotus, and it was not prepared for the changes to occur within its satisfying life.

Among the vibrant plants were ones that had reached the surface before the pink one and they were looked upon as the elders of the pond. All the citizens of the pond respected and honored the presence of the elders. Their wisdom was much valued and their majestic beauty admired by all. The change was so gradual that it was not immediately obvious to the other members of the community. The pink lotus was one of the first ones who noticed that one of the elders, gently swaying nearby, was not as vibrant as usual.

"Grandmother are you all right?" asked the concerned lotus. "I am just fine," came the gentle answer. "What is happening to your beautiful purple petals? Why are they starting to droop and wilt?" asked the pink lotus, which was beginning to worry.

The elder plant asked, "Do you remember what you felt when your leaves began to nourish your whole plant body and how you infused your whole being with the joyful and happy feelings of being blessed?"

"Yes, yes," replied the pink one. "It was such a wonderful sensation, as if I was drinking ambrosia and nectar from the heavens".

"Have you not noticed the changes in your root system and where it is anchored now?" asked the elder.

"I have not really paid attention to it, but now that you mentioned it, I have felt a change lately. Now that you have made me aware I would like to focus my awareness and check my root system," responded the pink lotus.

As the pink lotus withdrew its awareness it heard the Elder's last words, "Check the structure of your stalk while you are at it."

Pink lotus entered a meditative state and its spirit essence dove into the different layers below the surface. It had taken its life on the surface for granted and had not paid attention to its grounding parts below. It was stunned at the changes it encountered under the surface of the water. Its stalk had not only grown bigger and sturdier, but it had also lost its flexibility and was now as steady and strong as a tree trunk. The biggest change however, was at the base where the roots had formed a strong foundation within the muddy, anchoring space around it.

The mud where the root lay did not have the black darkness any longer. Rays of light were pulsing and beaming from the roots, illuminating and surrounding the area, and changing it into a different environment. The nourishing components that were hidden in the black mud now were revealed as golden particles of a honey-like substance, and the big, thick roots were harvesting this miracle grow effortlessly. The astonished awareness of the lotus realized that the skin, the bark of its trunk, was also emitting a glow that lit its path all the way to the surface. Not too far from its anchoring, glowing root was the niche where the elder's roots were housed. Pink lotus gasped in wonder for the elder's roots and stalk were not only glowing, but they were pulsing columns of white light forming a spiralling beam that pierced the darkness as it soared to the surface.

Its consciousness was about to return to the surface when it heard a small voice reaching out from below that said, "Hey, lady." Puzzled, pink lotus looked around and noticed a tiny seedling poking its baby tip out of a pile of muddy rocks. "Well hello little one, how are you?" asked Pink.

"I was scared at first but then I saw your light," the small tip answered. "This is a strange dark place, and you and the other one over there are the only ones glowing. How did you do that? Can I glow like you too?"

"Well, yes," Pink answered.

"Please, show me? Please Pink Lady?" the seedling begged.

"I must go now, but I will come back to tell you how to do it," Pink smiled at the little one's enthusiasm.

"Promise?" the little tip insisted. "I promise I will come back and help you find the way," pink lotus replied, and with that promise floating in the current, Pink lotus' spirit rose to the surface.

"Well?" The elder chuckled as it watched the questioning wonder within pink lotus.

"It is amazing, I had no idea," pink said wonderingly. "Why have you not told me about this part of our lives? Please grandmother, please tell me what is happening and why?"

"I have often tried to give you many clues, but you have never asked the questions until this moment. Now open your mind and listen to the story of creation," the elder began.

"As a seed you were sent down to explore the dark mud below. You were one of the brave and courageous ones who overcame your fears and worked hard at extracting the nutrients in the mud within your roots that are part of yourself. You discovered the hidden codes within your heart and rose to the surface with all the knowledge you gained from the experience of the muddy bottom layers. Upon reaching the surface, you embraced the new environment without fear and gave birth to your beautiful self, a lotus blossom. You embraced joy, happiness, and most important of all, you send out waves of thanksgiving. These are high frequencies of transformation, and when you immersed your whole plant-self in it, a circuit of light particles ignited within your structure and brought light into your stem and roots. Your roots could now sense with clarity and use the light particles to purify the dark mud into a golden food source.

"This specialty food source has been feeding me for a while and it will happen to you as well. This nectar of the Gods has nourished my being, and I am ready to enter the next stages of my life. I have gained and harvested the knowledge, wisdom, and experiences that my plant life has offered me, and I am ready to enter all of it into a new seed. Before the transformation can happen, I must release and detach from everything I have known, including my roots, my stem, my leaves and my beautiful petals. I do not need them any longer, for they have nourished me and given me a wonderful life. I do not know exactly where I am going, but my inner self knows that it will be a new pond of unlimited potentials where I could bloom as another most extraordinary lotus.

"You have all the information now and it is your responsibility to teach the young ones below that they too may choose to embrace the alchemy of transformation. Goodbye my beloved child. Pay attention, be my witness, and record everything that you see that it may be stored also within your core."

Pink lotus watched with mixed emotions as the elder's beautiful purple petals shrunk and fell into the water. From within the core of the blossom, a seed pod appeared. It was a very different and unusual pod, for it held only one seed. The pod itself was translucent, and a large crystal seed was shimmering within this cocoon. Suddenly, the pod was engulfed in a beam of light that rose from below. With an explosive, brilliant flash, the crystal seed was ejected high into the air. Pink lotus strained itself to see where it was going but no matter how hard it tried, it could only perceive a shining object moving further and further away. It was as if there was a bright star in the sky that suddenly blinked out of sight.

It was a strange day for Pink for it realized that the elder had given it a precious gift. It resolved to fulfil its promise to the young seedling below as soon as possible and knew that there would be no trace of the elder's roots in the mud any longer. Its passage and its presence would be but a memory held lovingly in the wisdom of the lotus. Pink accepted the fact that it had time to prepare without fear and knowing fully that it was to embark on another adventure soon. Its heart filled with love and thanksgiving for the elder, and Pink planned to pass on this wonderful message to all its friends and family members on the surface of the pond before its own inevitable departure.

The life cycle of the lotus is a mirror of the human cycle and an extraordinary gift of the Earth Mother. We are the human-lotus-seeds and have entered the darkness of the muddy bottom of a three-dimensional reality of duality. We are enclosed within our heavy thought patterns, our attitudes and our perceptions of the ego-self. The lotus is showing us the choices we have and the realization of the potentials that are waiting for us. The power of Alchemy was encoded within our DNA modules and it is now time to follow the path of the lotus, growing, breeching the dimensional barriers, and finally emerging on the surface of Light.

This is just the first step in our journey towards the ultimate surface. A deep-sea-diver knows that he has to rise slowly to the surface to survive the pressures of the water. He must be patient and allow himself to drift slowly upwards and surrender to the elements around him. In the same manner we must embrace patience and surrender to the elements within ourselves and the ones within our environment. The elder lotus reveals the potential of the next stages of transformation and it offers a parallel scenario for the human seed. From this platform of first awakening we have the opportunity to regain our memories, to accept our true membership within Divine Oneness and to project ourselves as the crystal seed into the next stage of evolution.

CHAPTER THREE

The Challenge of Chaos

The energy of chaos is but the fruit of change and its inevitable presence cannot be ignored. Einstein's statement," *Change is the only constant in the Universe*" can only add to the concept. The saga of the lotus and the analogy of the Mini-Miners, is only a shimmering, mirror reflection for what is in store for the human story. Imagine the chaos that is created when we have to evacuate and relocate a whole city to another continent, let alone a distant planet, with a different atmosphere.

The big move is now imminent, and the Earth, with all its occupants took the first step towards the necessary changes. The agreement of the Harmonic Convergence was the shot of the starter button and initiated the massive project of dismantling the old structures. The Earth and all its occupants are about to embark on an unprecedented voyage into unknown dimensional space. It cannot do so while still wearing a three dimensional suit. Every particle of the Earth has to be redesigned, and its body re-outfitted, to meet the required specification. Gaia, the Earth Mother has agreed to stay until the completion of the project and will assist wherever she can. Her knowledge, wisdom and creative powers are vital and essential in achieving this restructuring process. Based on the human time line, this humongous construction project might take years, even centuries for it is correlated to the choices of the Mass Consciousness Mind. In other words, it cannot be achieved in one life time. This incredible move has never happened before and has become the intense focus of observation by many other Beings in Space. The first notable evidence that something was happening occurred with the fall of the Berlin Wall in 1989. It was an unanticipated event in human history, and yet it ended the *cold war* between the two main players on the human board game. It brought in the infant tendrils of the potential of world peace within the warrior mind, and it was the starting shot that initiated the rise in consciousness.

Every scientific and engineering team was called to action due to all the changes happening all at once in different stages of every corner of the world. The Kryon team had completed the recalibration of the magnetic grid around the Earth into a higher vibrational frequency, and it was now ready for the next step. Once the magnetic frequencies were changed, a chain of events fell into place like a domino effect and the vibrations rippled and radiated out into all the Earth's realms. The magnetic poles showed the most noticeable shift first, followed by the more intense physical pole shifts. This caused movements of the tectonic plates, as they need to shift into new positions as well. The four elements soon slowly set the wheels of their seasonal changes in motion. They prepared for the arrival of the fifth element, the ethers, a high frequency element that flows within the fourth, fifth and other higher dimensional layers. The Earth's weather patterns, as discussed before, began shifting and adjusting in every corner of the world in order to help stabilize the whole structure at every step of the change. The pollution of all the four elements had an effect in that it accelerated and intensified the process. More violent storms, tornadoes and hurricanes would sweep across the globe in the following years. Rain and snow would fall in areas that had not seen such deluges and freezing weather for years. For the humans, it will seem as if the weather patterns had gone insane, and that the seasons had forgotten when and how they were to appear in different areas of the world.

Today evidence has shown that the Shift would also affect all the Earth kingdoms, especially the animal kingdom. The song birds were noticeably one of the first species to disappear and will slowly be followed by many other animals. Their living essence has returned to the pool of creation within the Earth, and there it will wait until the transformed Earth has reached a new home. The new dimensional environment will dictate the kinds of animals that can live here, and they will be born anew. The dolphins and the whales however, are an entirely different story. These intelligent mammals are the vehicles of another support team from a different dimensional place. Their interest in the human project caused these highly evolved beings to volunteer to store some of the information and knowledge that the human vessel could not. They kept the hidden files in safe keeping until such time that the potential of awakening would materialize. The Shift was the long awaited message that the human consciousness now has the capacity to receive the missing links and their work as librarians has come to an end. Having completed their mission most of them wish to return to their home-world. They purposely beach themselves with the help of the changing ley-lines in the ocean that confuses their internal guidance systems, helping them fulfill their wish.

The mineral kingdoms are also in the throes of change. The crystal kingdom has played an important role throughout the history of mankind and has performed many duties as storage units, energy channels and as crucial components in technology. They continue to be part of technology, but are now taking the roles of amplifiers that will support, amplify, enhance and strengthen the rising energies within the human-soul structure. For example, a healing crystal will increase and strengthen the resolve and effort of the human to heal itself. On the other side of the coin however, it will also amplify the efforts of the Ego, especially the Spiritual Ego. The Ego, as discussed earlier, is one of the anchoring systems wired into the human construct and when the crystals are used to support the Ego, it will only cause more confusion and chaos in the structure.

The Goddess then pointed out the challenges for the human kingdom. As we have realized, the human structure is the most intricately, sophisticated bio-computer program ever created. Multiple, unfathomable systems have been wired into this model that are yet to be discovered by human scientists. The most intriguing one is the dimensional factor within, and without the human vessel. Most of these layers are not visible to the three-dimensional human sight except for a few humans who carry the unusual gift of clairvoyance.

All anchors are to be lifted out of the main frame, and it presents a great challenge for the Soul-human being. The Ego is part of Duality, and Duality cannot function, nor exist within a higher dimensional framework. To ease the stress of the inevitable transition, a new component is being introduced into the strands of Duality, creating a transitional layer coined *Triality*. This new component begins to raise one's awareness that there is another option available to Free Will. Free Will remains as the special gift bestowed upon the human-Soul being as a tool, and it is the main deciding factor in every choice the human makes. This next option is the first step in accepting the understanding that there truly is no such thing as the opposing forces of good versus evil in the high mind of Creation. The questions that will arise in the questing human mind become, "Do you look at things as evil, or do you accept it as neither good nor bad, but as just *IS*? Can you begin to look at things not as black and white, but treat both as just great colors? Can you accept your life as a divine gift and not as a punishment? Will you choose to reach the understanding that human drama is a stage for Duality?"

Using white paint on a white canvas produces the same results as using black paint on a black canvas. It will be just a piece of unremarkable art. However, when both black and white are used in harmony, it displays a unique composition that would create an emotion of awe and delight. Triality will allow the mind to transcend Duality with the awakening sense that *'forgiveness and compassion'* are not part of the vocabulary of higher consciousness. In the eyes of our loving Creator, we, the Godlings are of pure, harmonious light and cannot do anything wrong. Therefore, the heavy energy of forgiveness does not and cannot exist, within the light of our being. The same energy envelops compassion. The emotion of compassion is of the lower frequency because it assumes that there is something wrong that needs our help. This emotion only feeds the control-ego body layer. The Goddess understands how difficult it is for us to jump these hurdles and she encourages us to take it slowly by moving into the emotion of detach-compassion as an initial step.

It is the nature of Duality to try to ostracise this new intrusion, and for many who reject the new member, it will only cause more chaos within all the biological layers. This is especially true of the emotional human mindset. The push-pull, opposing forces of duality have been battling each other since the beginning of time, but will naturally join forces to face the new comer. This new component is considered a threat to everything that is known, even to the familiar constant bickering opposing forces.

The positive side was shouldered by the Soul component, while the negative, heavier side was the human vessel's role to take. The third party arrived with the offer of neutrality and will, at first, be rejected by the Duality team. This confrontation will be faced by every human-Soul on the Earth plane as part of the restructuring program. In Earth years, this process can take many life times for those who are not ready to release and detach from the familiar heavy and dark emotional dramas enjoyed by many humans. It is the letting go of the comfort of the familiar old shoe, or ragged old blanket that can form a lifelong challenge.

Fear, as we know it, is the main supporting column of the Ego, and it feeds heavily on the energies of Chaos. Fear imprisons the mind and requires drastic, attention-getting measures to break free from the bars of this prison cell. The year 2000 came sliding in on the compounded fears of a Y2K technological meltdown. To everyone's surprise, nothing happened, for that specific glitch was a potential in the old time line. Fear and anxiety were replaced by relief and the world stepped into the year 2000 with the belief that, somehow that disaster was averted and that all was well. It was an illusion of the ego-mind, for the year 2000 heralded the beginning of the change. The preparations were in place and ready for the demolition teams to begin the dismantling of the old structures. Stripping away and removing an old husk will reveal the precious, living seed of light, giving it the opportunity to bloom with beauty and love.

With a sudden explosive, lightening strike, the Twin Towers in New York suddenly were no more, and Ground Zero was born in 2001. The two towers were the symbol of the two pillars of Duality and had to be demolished as part of the restructuring program. They were also the pedestals for the Mass Ego in which society showed a blatant disregard for the imbalance created by materialistic greed and obsession for economic dominance. From the dusty, painful chaos rose the anguished cry of thousands around the globe. *Nine-eleven* became a focus, a centrifuge that spiralled into waves of Triality-based emotions of compassion; love one's fellow man, and an awakening sense that we are all citizens of one planet who could choose to help each other. The numerous Souls that left that day had agreed to sacrifice their human lives for this specific purpose. In doing so, it created a space for new talented Souls to enter the human stage. The aftermath of this significant incident became another step towards changing the mass consciousness, for many felt as if the world they lived in had forever changed. The old familiar shoe had been discarded, and it left a feeling of uncertainty, discomfort, anxiety and a new layer of Fear.

Deep within the Earth's crust, the tectonic plates trembled and shifted, and once again the energy of Chaos descended in 2004 and enveloped the South-Eastern section of the globe. At least four countries experienced massive changes, not only environmentally, but also socio-economically. The Mass Mind was jarred back into compassion as awe of the power of the Four Elements stirred emotions globally. As the earth continued its compliance with the dismantling command of the higher powers, shock waves rolled in as Katrina struck New Orleans in

2005. Katrina was soon followed by the anguished cries of Japan in 2011 which reinforced the world's compassion and raised the consciousness of being part of one Earth family in need. It was the beginning of a worldwide change that would radiate throughout the universe.

In the meantime, another department had initiated a program of classifying the various levels of consciousness among the humans to minimize the traumatic effects of the Shift. The mediatory qualities of Triality would be the deciding factor for the category of each group.

Holographic realities, which I have coined as *holodecks*, were constructed as containment units. These are dimensional spaces of realities on the Earth plane and exist simultaneously with each other, occupying and intersecting the same spectrum of space as we know it. It is not an easy concept for the human brain, and the Goddess encouraged us to open our minds to the possibility of it. Once again, she asked us to keep in mind that *everything* has to change, and until we can meet those requirements, we must remain in the holodecks for our own safety.

Groups of people with roughly the same level of consciousness were assigned holodecks where they could evolve and transform at their own pace, based on the choice of Free Will. Each deck contained different levels as well, to provide maximum choices for the inhabitants. For example those who were still wrapped in the warrior energies and who chose to continue with the emotions of hatred, revenge, retaliation and other war-like emotions, were held in their holodeck unit. Within this space of existence, they could continue to play out their roles on the stages of war and animosities. Those who chose to play a more moderate level of violence would then occupy a different scenario within this warrior deck.

Others who wished to remain within the dormant state of unawareness would complete their lives with their daily itinerary of a job and various entertainments for their amusements. The population at this level are the ones who would not be aware of any extraordinary events happening. They chose to remain oblivious of the Great Shift and wished to complete their life cycle as it was before. Bear in mind that all the decks are constructed within the Earth-ship and will travel with it as it blasts off into its voyage. Imagine a cruise ship with many decks on board. As the ship sails away every passenger has been assigned their cabins on different deck levels according to their tickets. The passengers are free to interact with their fellow deck mates during the voyage as everyone on board is transported to the same destination.

The ones who have chosen to begin their paths of awakening and enlightenment would occupy another holo-reality where they could find many teachers, healers, counsellors and etheric guides to assist them in an accelerated program. These are those who call themselves the *Lightworkers,* and they too, exist in different levels within their designated holo-realities according to their states of evolution of consciousness.

Just like the decks on the cruise ship, these realities exist on the same plane. This means that someone on the accelerated plane could still be aware of everything that is happening on the other levels. It becomes a choice of whether one would turn on the TV and watch the news, go to a ballgame, or participate in a meditation class.

There is a constant flow of movements between the realities to allow for changes in the level of Consciousness of each individual. These holodecks will be maintained and monitored by a specific group of angelic light beings to provide the stability needed within the rising flow of consciousness. However, there are a few factors to consider in this system. The occupants of a lower frequency Consciousness cannot understand what is happening at the higher levels and will often blank out, ignore or even detach from the glimpses they might catch. This anomaly will affect friendships and relationships of any kind between the members of the different levels. This could be a challenge for many lightworkers unless they accept the neutralizing concept of Triality, which is embracing the fact that there is *No-thing wrong, No-thing broken, No-thing needs fixing* and that everything that is happening is just *IS.* Assuming that we know what is best for someone else, and insisting on implementing or forcing a change of behavior on them, will immediately lock us into one level, preventing us from moving into another level. Detaching from all drama and entering a state of surrendered, meditative, stillness of the mind is one of the entry tickets into the *spiritual first class deck.*

The Spiritual Ego plays a major role at this level for it feeds on the emotion of self-aggrandisement. There are many who came with strong psychic gifts such as clairvoyance and clairaudience at birth. During the last century, many have been exulted, honored and their lives put on a pedestal as Gurus. The word Guru basically was another word for teacher, however with time, it was used in a different fashion. Their persona was exhibited as powerful, their lives glamorous, and for some, financially extremely profitable. As part of the Shift, the word Guru has to return to the energy of G.U.R.U—*Gee You Are You,* bringing the focus back to the SELF.

The art of channelling any entity and the ability of mediumship became a coveted ability and sought after by numerous lightworkers. It was all part of the game and played well by every psychic participant. With the onset of the Great Shift, this scenario too has to undergo the process of change. No one is exempted from the restructuring program. No gift will be taken away or recalled but each gifted one is encouraged to raise the frequency of the gift into the resonating vibration of the self. The gift came on the current of Duality where the spiritual Ego has a free hand, and at its present frequency cannot enter the new levels. Throughout human history it is a given that embracing a new concept that does not follow the old customary way is very difficult and, at times not possible, to embrace within one lifetime. It is a dilemma for those entrenched in the old way of using their psychic gifts and who believed that it was a reliable guidance as to how they live their lives.

The Spiritual Ego is fully aware of the inevitable change that will affect its dominant role, and it is in full warrior gear. It is a powerful strand, very subtle in its ways, and often undetectable by many lightworkers. It has indulged, enjoyed and wrapped itself in the illusion of the Guru-power for centuries. Like all the other ego layers, it cannot be terminated but has to be reconfigured as well, and given a different role to play. Instead of the dominant, controlling, egocentric position, it could become the energy source to propel the human vessel into an enlightened and aware spiritual personality. With his life, Jesus gave us the first clues as to how to confront the Ego-self. The question, *"What would Jesus do?"* has merit and could provide a strong guiding line for many spiritual seekers.

The new mandates were in place and fully functioning as the Earth marched into 2012. Every change was first implemented in the etheric stratum and thus not visible or even noticeable to the unawakened human sight. It was clear at this point that the changes were finally noticed, and adhered to, by those who chose to enter the Path to Unity Consciousness.

The elements as instructed continued their reconfiguration of the weather patterns around the world. Forest fires, draughts and unusual floods like the one that materialized in New York were reported on every continent. Meanwhile, the Earth's crust continued to undulate like a serpent sending rippling tremors along its surface as it shrugs out of the old suit in preparation for the journey into the Unknown regions of interdimensional space. The energies of chaos will continue to roam all corners of the world until the construction sites have been cleared and we have reached safe harbor in a new neighborhood.

CHAPTER FOUR

The Enigma of 2012

To the disappointment of many who mired themselves into the fear-based mode of Duality, Armageddon did not happen. The Earth did not end and no one or thing was obliterated as predicted. It was the end of the old way of living, as well as the end of the old customs, belief systems and habits. It was the entrance of a new era for humanity as a new Earth was being reconstructed to herald Peace among Men and awareness of its membership as a world citizen. The spiritual communities of the world had accepted and embraced the reality that the Earth had shifted and was hurdling towards a plane of higher consciousness. We, the passengers on this spaceship Earth, were now required to adjust ourselves in order to gain entrance into this new plane.

As we stepped into 2012, the waves of Armageddon resurfaced with a vengeance among the fearful throng. Contradictory messages ranged from the possibility of three days of darkness, massive black outs, devastating tsunamis and earthquakes to mass awakening from an unnatural sleep into instant enlightenments. The perplexing situations were boiling in a cauldron spiced with uncertainty and uneasiness. Some even expected everyone to fall into a deep asleep one day and awaken the next morning fully enlightened.

Anxiety mounted within many factions of those who monitored the Earth changes, and who began to preach the notion of the End Times to the vulnerable public. The media quickly took advantage and jumped on the band-wagon with related movie productions, talk shows and interviews. It became a drama of a feeding frenzy as the baffling chaos and anxiety gave rise to people spending their life-savings to buy special shelters and hoard survival items in their basements. The hopeful messages of the Mayan Calendar, which stressed that it was only the end of a universal cycle and that the Earth was due to enter another one, did not alleviate the waves of fear and panic.

The dates of 12-12-12, December twelve of the year 2012 was considered a significant numerical date. Many believed that we had reached our destination on that date. Others based this belief upon another date, that of December 21st of 2012. Many groups focussed their attention upon these two dates, and in doing so a vortex of energy swirled around these times. In one of his sermons Jesus announced that, *"When two or more come together in my name there I will be also."* The human mind is one of the powerful tools gifted to the Soul-human being and when a number of humans focus their intention on a specific target it generates a powerful beam of etheric energy. This is evident when many discovered the power of combined prayers of prayer circles or group meditations. On the other side of the scale were, of course the opposing masses who claimed that it was all a hoax and dismissed the strange behaviors of their supposedly crazed fellow humans.

The main stream populace were unaware that Spaceship Earth had already launched its etheric layers into the dimensional sea by the year 2012. It was a new beginning for the Earth and all its inhabitants. What we as humans have not understood until recently was that everything begins at the unseen etheric layers. This applies not only to the Earth's auric fields but also to the human etheric body layers. Existing within our holodecks, we are not aware of the Shift, and we assume what we perceive with our senses to be the physical reality we live in. As a huge planet body, the physical Earth cannot be transported through the dimensional currents safely without preparations. Its etheric parts will begin the journey and clear a corridor for the physical Earth to follow in easy stages, as it is being towed slowly through on powerful etheric tractor beams. The changes and the restructuring programs will continue as the Earth travels through the inter-dimensional sea.

Visual confirmations have been detected more frequently through various high technical instruments as validation that something unusual is happening. For the past few years, strange and puzzling anomalies in space have been detected by many space monitoring agencies and these were increasingly visible through the powerful lenses of massive telescopes. What was happening on the surface of the sun resulted in more attention and increased surveillance. Waves of Gama rays were rising beyond normal levels, and ionic storms and sun flares were not following its normal recorded paths. These irregular energy fluctuations affected the electronic mechanisms all over the globe, and at times would play havoc with our computers and other communication systems.

The subtle result of magnetic pole shifts also made itself felt in many electrical circuits and instruments. Radar units and compasses had to be recalibrated constantly, especially in air traffic navigation. The ley lines within the Earth's magnetic grid have taken other routes and brought confusion in the migrational pathways for many animals. Ley lines are energy lines similar to unseen electrical flows that intersect the Earth's surface, creating grid-like pathways. Migrating animals use the lines as guiding systems to reach their customary destinations. Because of the rerouting of these lines, many birds have been found lost and floundering in different areas. Ley lines were not the only strands changing their patterns. Vortexes of energy in specific areas of the world that were valued and carefully monitored by spiritual groups began to shift their locations. For example, the much revered center in the Himalayas shifted, and waves of etheric energy emerged spiraling in Chile, a country located in South America. These energetic centers have always been considered sacred places by the indigenous local population and this belief system has been embraced by those who are sensitive to the more intense vibrations emitted from the core of these vortexes.

Reading the subtle messages of the stars is an ancient art and is still valued today by those who have made it their lives' study. For the astronomers, astrologers, and enthusiastic star-gazers, there were interesting sights to behold. Planetary alignments that had not been recorded for eons of time were happening in the sky. The star systems seemed to be shifting as well, and interested astrologers found that they had to recalculate many of their charts. The configuration of the Star of David that was depicted as the Christmas star made its appearance in the sky once more. This time, it would not herald a special birth, but perhaps to awaken a new group of Magi who might choose to follow its brilliant message across the heavens. Messages were being sent for interested parties to watch the skies, for there would come a time when the changes would become visible to the naked eye. The borealis, known as the Northern lights, have decorated the Northern skies with its mesmerizing dance since the beginning of time. With the change upon us, it only became more spectacular. Readings on many technological instruments that had been monitoring various frequencies around the Earth's atmosphere noticed slight discrepancies and unusual fluctuations.

Throughout this auspicious year, the weather continued to play their unpredictable patterns around the globe. The ice cap in the north continued to melt with the rise in temperatures, while the world governments continued to argue and debate the cause of global warming. It was a year of instability, erratic fluctuations, unpredictability and a type of purging in many aspects of human life. Within the macro-world, the economy entered erratic instability and previously stable countries suddenly faced the unheard of reality of bankruptcy. A number of large financial empires tumbled, and proud barons of extreme wealth, who held the monopoly of trade for generations, fell off the board. Nothing could be hidden any longer, and scandal upon scandal of unacceptable behaviors of prominent figures in society faced public outrage upon exposure. Covert acts of corruption that were ignored, over-looked or hidden were brought to light for more and more people found the courage to speak out against these dark behavior patterns.

2012 was the grand opening year of the biggest spiritual shopping mall ever constructed, for it provided multiple choices in any direction for anyone interested in pursuing their spiritual growth. Numerous spiritual retreats, workshops and seminars became available providing an extensive smorgasbord of a variety of topics. Excuses of unavailability were no longer acceptable. Motivational speakers seemed to rise out of the woodwork and were advertising their views on the Media. The communication and information networks were saturated with news related to the Great Shift. On the other hand, many traditional churches were scrambling for worshippers as the wave of spirituality seemed to gain momentum since the Harmonic Convergence. Members seem to be dissatisfied and were searching for something that they were not even sure of what it was they were looking for. The component of the internal spiritual guidance system of the world population had been activated. The word *Ascension,* the hidden code, the password had been entered into the mainframe of the Mass Mind and cannot be deleted.

All of a sudden words such as yoga, meditation, channelling and mediumship are acceptable vocabulary in daily conversations. Yoga studios can be found almost in every neighborhood. Energy healing techniques such as Reiki, Therapeutic Touch and Healing Touch are slowly recognized as beneficial and even allowed in certain hospitals. Alternative medicine such as acupuncture grew into more prominence as society became more consciously aware that everyone has the right to make individual choices regarding their health issues. At the same time controversial strands were swirling in and out of every new idea supporting the constant motion of duality. One day butter was bad to have and margarine was a healthier choice. Overnight the messages seemed to reverse itself and butter was considered the better choice. Then meat consumption decreased as a vegetarian diet was promoted to be a much better way of life. Herbal medicine sales escalated causing frantic opposing data from the pharmaceutical groups. The erratic swing of the pendulum of emotions kept many people on edge as the contradictory messages pushed and pulled, creating more confusion, opening the door to the feeling of hopelessness and a sense of *giving up*. The energies of Duality were shaken out of its comfortable track.

It was an unusual year of fluctuating waves of energy that affected every walk of life. Planetary retrogrades were creating havoc for those who were etherically sensitive and caused emotional and physical trauma in their daily lives. There were reports of increased psychosis among the mentally ill and even a sense of going crazy within the spiritually gifted community. In addition, the invisible rays that rippled down through space from extreme sun-flares, ionic space storms and the planetary alignments continued to affect the world's communication systems and all electronic devices.

December 2012 heralded the end of this unsettling year and the majority hoped that the future would bring better news. On the twelfth day, spiritual ceremonies were held in numerous locations all over the globe. They were ceremonies of celebration for the participants understood that it was the beginning for exciting changes to come. The ceremonies were repeated on the twenty first as it was considered to be another date of entry into a new age.

The emotion of Anticipation was followed by impatience as the year drew to an end. There was a final *click* as if a door was closed and locked into place providing closure to the experiment begun eons ago within earth's linear time and space.

New questions surfaced after this unsettling year. What will happen next? What is in the future for humanity? How will the earth changes affect not only the environment but human life as we know it? As a world society what are we going to do about it? Will Aliens from outer space appear among us at last?

Once again controversial debates were flung back and forth in an effort to create an understanding in the Mass Mind. Some groups belief that, as a unit we have already ascended and only need to implement the new Universal laws of enlightenment. Others followed the notion that we are on the verge of entering the age of spiritual awakening. A very determined faction claimed that a number of its members have already reached the Promised Land within the fifth dimensional space. Meanwhile amongst all the talk the majority of earth's population continue to live their lives the way they are familiar with, following their customs, habits and daily routines.

PART THREE

The Ladder of Evolution

CHAPTER ONE

Perception.

The repeated message of the Goddess echoed in my mind as I listened to the spiritual conversations billowing around me. "Everything, I mean, everything must change before you can progress into the next stages of transformation and climb the next rung on the ladder of human evolution." She shared with us the message that the next three years after 2012 will be a time of choices, of massive changes that require challenging adjustments to all our senses. Our thought patterns and our perceptions of our lives emit powerful energetic waves and form the ebb and flow of our emotions. These in turn, affect our physical wellbeing. Lack of knowledge is one of the factors that tend to cloud our perceptions and create a resistance to anything new and unusual.

Imagine a person living in a hut in the Amazon jungle who suddenly has to face a construction crew that is about to demolish his home and build a twenty-first century luxurious home in its place. The familiar perception of his life is destroyed, and he has to face a tsunamic wave of multiple emotions of fear, chaos, uncertainty, grief and anger. Insisting that he move into this strange home with all the modern appliances right away would be overwhelming emotionally and mentally. He could potentially lose touch with his reality, becoming mentally unstable and deemed insane.

We are facing the same scenario as we enter the Great Shift and begin our first steps of the evolution of Consciousness. Our perceptions of the reality we have lived with require a reprogramming, for the changes are not always as obvious. The process often begins at the unconscious level and becomes more deliberate as we progress along the journey.

Our Soul partners are aware of the dangers of allowing the dimensional veils to lift too quickly. The Human Mass-Mind cannot absorb and process the massive changes if and when it is presented too fast in human terms. Yet, even with the monitored pace, there will be humans whose mind-perceptions cannot accept the influx of constant change. As a result, a chemical imbalance in the brain could manifest, and they could require medical attention for the rest of their lives.

For those who bravely make the choice of taking that first leap, we begin by taking down the hut. It is not an easy process but it can be accomplished with courage, tenacity, trust and faith in our soul connection and acceptance of our inner Divine-Self. We have been given all the time we need to prepare at our own speed and to process each change, step by step, and life-time after life-time, if necessary.

Through choice of Free Will, the energy of transmutation will accelerate and progressively intensify and be felt throughout the physical body. Initially, it will feel strange and uncomfortable, like a new pair of shoes. There could be periods of pain and may result in resistance and increase waves of fear, discomfort and disharmony within.

The first important step is to accept the fact that all the changes are happening all at once within all our layers, seen and unseen, by the naked eye. Linear thinking does not work any longer and the mind must begin the restructuring by acknowledging the reality of dimensional etheric space.

As we work on changing our physical structures, it will affect our mental, emotional and spiritual selves at the same time in all the dimensional layers we occupy. The waves of transforming energies form a powerful current of the ocean of the Unified Field of Consciousness. Unresolved congestions formed by old blockages of customs, fixed belief systems and built up fears, form a dam that will have a physical manifestation when it bursts. The continual accelerating forces of the consciousness-energy cannot be stopped, and the pressures of this Divine Force will eventually break through, dislodging any low-frequency consciousness. Resistance is truly futile in this scenario.

The hut, of course, is the metaphor that represents our biology and forms the starting point of the process. A highly evolved home requires a lot of power and therefore needs a bigger and more sophisticated electrical panel. The human construct was built with a panel we know as the Chakra system. In the ancient Sanskrit tongue the word Chakra means Wheel and it is anchored in the etheric spinal column. It is important to study and comprehend the function of our power panel, the

Chakra wiring system, in order to begin the restructuring program. The energy current that flows in this system is known as the Kundalini fire, for it creates flaming heat when it rises through the prana tube. When activated, the Kundalini rises like the legendary Phoenix, flaming with the celestial fires that bring in purification, initiation and rebirth into a higher vibration.

The chakra system forms our main circuitry, and it is the junction point that connects biology to Divine Soul source. The chakra panel supports seven rotating wheels and because it is not visible nor felt by human biology it is imperative to persuade the stubborn, lower mind that it truly exists. This power panel form the core, the foundation of the human structure, and everything is wired into this system. The current of power that runs through the whole power grid is contained within an energetic pipe-like structure we recognize as the prana tube. The word prana, also known as Chi energy, refers to the etheric energy flow within our being.

Energy flows like water and the wheels keep the energy currents flowing and energizing the whole body. Imagine seven pools interconnected by canals. In the center of each pool there is a spinning fan-like water wheel that keeps the water aerated and flowing from one pool to the next. When a lot of debris begins to clog the canals, the water is blocked from flowing into the next pool and the water current begins to slow down. As more and more flotsam collects in the pool it will stick to the fins, or spokes of the water-wheel, and slows down its rotation. Slowly the water becomes more and more stagnant if the pool is not cleansed. Pretty soon all the pools appear sickly and lifeless.

The chakra system works in the same manner. The debris that clogs the channels are the heavy, dark emotions we hold onto and unless released and healed it results in an imbalanced system causing physical illnesses. Deep Fears, repressed traumas and dramas that have not been integrated, faced and experienced are pushed down into the substrata of the emotional mind slowing the chakra turbine even more. There are cone-like spokes within each Chakra Wheel that form spinning energy columns both front and back of the body and these are programmed to keep spinning throughout our life time. It cannot stop spinning and will labour to keep its rotation by drawing a lot of energy from different parts of the body to achieve this. The chakras can only terminate its efforts upon physical death when the Soul leaves the human vehicle.

For Electrical currents to function it has to flow in a circuitry and stay connected to a source of power. The human belief that we are all separate is an illusion for we are all connected to the most intricate, powerful electrical circuitry called Divine Unity Consciousness of Oneness. The illusionary perception of separation was wired into the human construct as an anchor into the sea of Duality. However, there is another perception amongst many humans that tends to distort the idea of Oneness. Many feel that Oneness means the loss of individuality and the wrenching away of personal power. There is a fear of losing oneself and the disappearance of individual distinctions. This is not the case within the Universal Truth of Unity Consciousness of Ultimate Source. Within the Oneness, we are all members of a Divine Family. It is a family that recognizes the interconnectedness and interrelatedness of Souls, and that of all beings, and all aspects of creation. However, each retains its unique individual characteristics. When we begin to change our perception from being a victim, to a fully conscious spiritual adult who takes full responsibility for every act, every thought and emotion, it will open the intuitive mind to the true concept of Oneness.

The mature mind begins to perceive the illusions of Fear, begins to dissolve and release the fear-based dramas that were anchored within the subconscious blocks. Some of the blockages are energetic scar tissue of emotions that have been dealt with but not completely eradicated from the subconscious strata. These feel as if the painful drama has resurfaced. Trying to ignore or rebury this dark energy may cause more discomfort and pain within the biology.

"One does not become enlightened by imagining figures of light but by making the darkness conscious." Carl Jung

Everything within and around us vibrates. All components of the human structure contain filaments that intertwine with other vibrational strands spiralling together within columns of energy. These encompass vibrations of, not only the senses such as sounds, sights, smells and touch but also of all the elements. The vibrations of musical notes play a very important part for the higher frequencies of sound can travel through all the elements and touch all the senses.

A great percentage of the world's population sees our lives as the ultimate reality, and that it is the only *real life* for all of us. The major challenge for humanity is to accept that parts of us exist in a different reality and that the human perception is that of an illusionary, sophisticatedly created game-board.

CHAPTER TWO

The Ego Mantra

The Goddess keeps reminding us that this journey would not be as easy as we thought and that it would take many reincarnations to complete the reconstruction program. Each bar, each wall, each obstruction is subject to the demolition and the constrictive Duality box must be dismantled layer by layer.

The strongest and most complicated bar or anchoring system is the presence of the Ego. It is encoded in every strand of our structure and it cannot be removed, but can only be transformed in conjunction with all our layers. Everything is connected and wired together forming one complicated grid within our human structure. In order to face and transform every aspect of the Ego, we must examine our emotional, mental and spiritual layers. Changes in one system affect all the others, for it is a coordinated intricate communication system linked by the DNA spirals.

Every Ego layer thrives on drama and feeds upon the emotions that it creates. The Ego's resistance against change becomes more intense as we are continually bombarded with ray after ray of the energies of transmutation and transformation. Transforming each part of it into a higher frequency with the words of light and love is the first steps on the evolution ladder. Therefore, we must examine the role of the Ego and study its structure before we can begin to tackle any other section. Looking at the process from a different angle we may perceive it as a type of mutation of the human structure.

The success rate of the rewiring of the chakra system strongly depends on the capability of the individual to face the Ego. First of all, it can be a very difficult road for many to accept the presence of the Ego within the human character. It is part of human biology and it becomes as familiar as an arm or a leg to be used daily, often without much thought. It becomes a reflex action to hit back when we think that we are attacked either with words or with physical blows. "*An eye for an eye*" is a favorite mantra of the Ego. Jesus tried to show us the healing strand when he encouraged his disciples to "*turn the other cheek*". By this act alone, we temper the Ego-self with the wisdom gained that trying to heal violence with violence will only perpetuate the aggression.

The Ego has two faces, a positive and a negative outlook. Both sides are as effective in controlling human behavior patterns. One side's objective is to become a robe of glory, while the other side wants to wrap itself in a mantle of victimization. Both ultimately define the personality of the person wearing it. It often becomes an instant choice when faced with different dramas in life and can see-saw from one to the other without much thought. Both sides constantly battle for supremacy and can plunge the human psyche into an up-and-down see-saw of emotions.

The battle of the Self within the constraints of Duality becomes the feeding ground of the Ego. When faced with harsh survival issues, it dons the victim robe and decorates it with numerous words of darkness, such as anger, resentment, jealousy, low self-esteem, the poor-me attitude and even hatred. The belief that it is vitally important to gain material wealth to ensure a happy life is encouraged by the Ego. The Ego's portrayal of a happy, luxurious lifestyle continuously bombards our senses with unending mantras of, "Money gives me love. Money buys happiness. Money ends my suffering. Money makes my family love me more. Money is my ultimate goal. I deserve to have as much as my neighbor. It is not my fault; the world owes me."

For those who possess material wealth, it becomes a pedestal. It is an illusionary elevation of self-importance and a state of, "I am better because I have more money". No matter what side of the coin, it thickens the notion of separation. The Ego's main mantra is in support of separation as in: "*I am not my brother's keeper,*" which opens the door to selfishness and self-centeredness and not self-love.

When we choose to don the cloak of the Warrior we give the Ego a free pass to enter and embroil the Self in the mud-hole of emotions that are fully controlled by fear, anger and the need for retaliation and revenge. We emphasize the Ego's qualities once more as we examine our responses to almost anything that we perceive as a demeaning judgement, a criticism or anything that resembles an attack on the Shadow-Self. It is not in the Ego's nature to turn the other cheek, and we immediately initiate a form of counter-attack with stronger words of anger, hatred or violent physical actions in order to redeem our Ego-Self importance.

Those dark words and actions are as painful for the resident Soul and dim its light as if its clothes have become soiled. When the Soul leaves the physical body, it cannot leave the lower Earth Realms until it is cleansed. The act of cleansing in this case, is the process of metamorphoses by applying the acceptance and loving wisdom of the Soul as a means of transforming the dark garment into light. The Soul is the spiritual alchemist who holds the formula of transformation. Ultimately, love energy is the only component of alchemy that can alter vibration into a higher state. When the Soul decides to reincarnate before the healing process has been completed, it will return with its own personal '*dirty laundry*,' so to speak, with a more challenging script for its life.

As we enter the Great Shift, this level of Consciousness is one of the main challenges on the ladder of evolution, for no one can take the next step when we are still chained with the Ego-anchor. The Ego relishes human dramas, particularly that of suffering or hero-ship. Although we deny it loudly, humans enjoy telling their stories of suffering or hero-action to anyone who happens to be an available audience. In the telling and retelling of the stories, we elevate ourselves to the position of the hero, or the main character of suffering, and become addicted to movies or books that would satisfy this part of the Ego. Within the level of suffering lie numerous layers that are connected to Survival issues such as lack of material wealth, lack of health and lack of basic living needs. The energy of suffering when accepted with understanding and the surrender to the Higher-Soul-Self has the potential of an acceleration of Spiritual growth. When we invoke and allow the purity of Soul-Light to infuse our thoughts and emotions we begin to perceive suffering as an opportunity to heal ourselves at the deeper levels of our being.

The Spiritual Ego is one of the last layers to enter the chamber of transfiguration, for it is the most challenging layer. It was mentioned earlier that psychic abilities have been detected within many energetically sensitive individuals. Many grew into sages, prophets, gurus and even elevated to Sainthood. The Mass Mind worshiped these perceived higher advanced spiritual teachers and leaders as a means of reaching enlightenment. This special group was even considered to be Holy and worthy of being bowed down to, as they were set upon pedestals of honor, befitting a holy presence among us. The opulence and wealth that could possibly result from these positions would only increase the energies of jealousy and resentment. It became inevitable throughout the ages that the Spiritual Ego would focus so much on these worshipping energies that it would be coveted by the individual human mind.

More and more humans have begun the awakening process and have sampled the intoxicating euphoria of spiritual awareness. Initially, the initiates embraced the old belief systems that suggest that they must chant and meditate for hours in order to reach the valued state. Additionally, when told to protect themselves against psychic attacks or evil energies, they created walls of light around themselves. These protective shields were necessary before, but when we signed the agreement of the Harmonic Convergence, this type of protection built with the components of fear was no longer necessary. By accepting the possibilities and potentials of an attack, one gets locked in the Duality of the dark shadows of Ego-Fear, which does not match the vibrational frequencies of the Higher Consciousness. Imagine locking yourself in a strong glass box. No one can come in to attack you, but at the same time you cannot reach out for help or allow the Love energy to enter through the barrier.

The New-Aged Spiritual persona is persuaded to enter a state of initial knowingness, not realizing that it is often the illusionary veils of the Spiritual-Ego. The temptation of immediately stepping in the shoes of the Guru, teacher, healer or preacher can be overwhelming. When not acknowledged the Spiritual-Ego-Self grows into self-importance, establishing a belief system of, *"Us versus them"*. It is another level of separation, for it creates a chasm between those who have awakened and those who have not. When we insist on maintaining this belief system we continue to exist in the appropriate *'spiritual holodeck'* and any perceived growth would be but a stronger illusion of the Ego.

Spiritual competition is another heavy anchoring chain, for its subtlety can often be undetected by a Lightworker. The drive for the Lightworker to create abundance for one's self is overshadowed by the fear of competition. The competitive nature of the Ego indulges in this emotion, striving even harder to create the flow of material wealth. The Ego justifies each action as, *"I deserve this, I should be compensated for what I do"*. This level of competition, when not curbed or released, begins to be blanketed with increasing fear-based mentalities. We fear that others might steal, rob and use spiritual materials we lay claim to. The term *copy-right* begins to stalk our fear-based dreams, and dark words of resentment, jealousies and animosities permeate our wakening thoughts. We have difficulty working together or form partnerships with others when our vibrations do not resonate any longer at any level, spiritually or otherwise.

The Ego cloaks and coats every emotion and every thought pattern to justify its actions by claiming that it is love-based. It will twist and turn, and use every method possible to remain in control for at its root it knows that its days are numbered the moment the agreement to the Great Shift in Consciousness came into being. It takes on the role of a stubborn child who had been spoiled and allowed to control the household and now realizes that all of its privileges are about to be terminated. Every child is born into the world with a clean slate and is open to be taught to hate or to love. Only when the child is gently guided with love into a responsible adult, he or she will then be able take the position of a valuable contributing member of the family and of society.

The Ego has been the driving force behind every human player, and it is now time for the human to take over the role of a main contributor. Imagine that you are in charge of a starship and that you have given the Ego the position of commander. The Ego had occupied your captain's chair for a long time, and you went along with all its decisions because you believed that you were not capable or qualified to take the leading role. It is a false notion of unworthiness perpetuated by the constant whispers of the Ego. Then one day you realize that you have lost control of your own ship, and you wake up with the realization that you are capable and now want to regain your rightful power. You order the Ego out of the chair so that you can take over command of the steering wheel. At first, the Ego complies by standing beside the chair, insisting that you need its experience as a commander and wants to remain as an advisor. Nothing will change if you agree to this proposal. To get the Ego off the control bridge, you have to step into your power and firmly order it to take its new position in the engine room to provide more power for your ship.

This is a tug of war that is really crucial, for when the Ego embraces its job as the engineer; it will provide the power for your starship to accelerate into speed of light. You truly begin to walk the path of a Spiritual Adult who takes charge of your own choices with full responsibility. Your voice will proclaim without hesitation "*I AM* ". You begin to accept the membership into the ONENESS of all things with the support of the transformed Ego that declares: "*I know who I am and I claim my birthright of the love and wisdom of the Soul.*" The Dalai

Lama phrased this awareness with, *"I am and I am not,"* completely surrendering to his Higher Self and moving into the position of his power of *I AM* and not the *little i* of the Ego. Another Spiritual philosopher clarified his understanding with *"I can only be a Somebody when I am a Nobody."* With that statement, he clearly understood that once he demotes the Ego to the position of a No-body can he claim his rightful role as a *Somebody* who is able to walk the path of an Enlightened Being.

There is no protection needed for any being that blazes and shines with the Light of Love, for no speck of darkness can exist or attach itself to a beam of light. As the light within increases its strength, the candle flame of the **little-i-ego** dims and will eventually be completely absorbed by the blinding flame of Unity-Creator-Consciousness of the residing Soul.

The acquired vibrational frequency of the Light filaments of Unity Consciousness is the final crystal-key that opens the gate to our destination of ascension. A radiating and blazing Soul-Light is the only light that will reveal the true nature of Duality and the Ego anchor.

CHAPTER THREE

Rewiring the Panel

In the old system the multiple cone-like-fans within each Chakra Wheel called petals, spin constantly, functioning like a generator. The Chakras are like the fuses in an electrical panel and are connected forming a circuit that loops around connecting to the Earth at one point and to the crown on top of the head at the other point. This phenomenon is known as the golden, egg-shaped energy container that spins around the physical body with a magnetic pole at each end. The poles are the Earth-Star, connecting to the Earth core, and the Soul-Star connecting to the inter-dimensional Source, completing the circuit of power. This system has to be rewired into a new circuit with the heart as the core. The heart is not only the holder of the Christ Seed-of-Light, but it is also an inter-dimensional gate that was dormant for most of us until now. The wiring within all the chakras has to be re-routed and connected to the higher vibrations of the gate. In order to do this, the wiring has to be compatible and match the frequency of the gate. The heart, in turn becomes the headquarters, the main control center, and the central conduit that oversees the new system. Our Heart Chakra has close similar functions as the Earth's Heart Chakra. Both are main entrance points for Divine Creative Love energies that stimulate the manifestation of Creation.

The Root Chakra

We begin with the three lower chakras, for they form the foundation layer of the human construct. The First Chakra, known as the Root, is situated at the base of the spine and it is linked to the Earth element. The Root is also the acknowledgement of our grounding connection to the Earth's magnetic grid, and its particles are programmed with the unique special gifts, attributes and qualities that were recorded in the Akash. Therefore, it deals with accumulated fear-based strands of separation, survival and abandonment. The Root also is the placement of the male sexual organ energetic layers and the lower endocrine organs.

This Chakra has four cone-shaped petals and rotates with the frequency of the color RED and vibrates with the musical Key of low C. In its congested situation, it is perceived to have dark, black blobs floating inside and it has a discordant note. Keep in mind that the dark filaments of Fear overseen by the Ego are the ingredients that form the basis of congestion that permeate every layer of the human framework. To promote clarity of the chakra energies, I have included the words found in the *Sound of Music.* For the Root we hear, *"Doe, a deer, a female deer"* sung in low C. The doe represents the energy of Fear and survival issues. She is deeply connected to the Earth and the forest, and yet she is wrapped in the anxiety of survival for herself and her children.

To release the blockages in this center, we must face the inner fears and anger of the emotions involved. Allowing the Ego-Self to persuade us to indulge in self-pity and the effort of avoiding the Shadow-Self only prolong the inevitable dam-burst. The first key word to unravel the old circuits is *Forgiveness.* This powerful word is a bridge across the Duality Mind, and it is antagonistic to the Ego for the Ego-Will opposes its application with full strength. Forgiving others is an easier act for most of us. On the other hand, the act of self-forgiveness requires a very strong mindset and the will to change, for the bars of guilt and shame are steel traps of the Ego-Mind.

When a child is in the womb, it is cocooned within a safe, warm, watery world and is soothed by the Mother's heartbeat. However, within this cocoon the baby is subjected to the Mother's emotional state and receives its first imprints of either positive or negative vibrations. The trauma of birth is the next imprint of separation and abandonment that every baby has to go through. The baby is suddenly, and often violently, torn from a safe world and expelled into a strange and frightening new world of heaviness. These imprints form the deepest 'roots' within the first Chakra and it is an essential priority step towards the dismantling process. After the trauma of birth, the child's emerging Consciousness is like a sponge that craves the energies of being nurtured, the safe harbor of belonging and unconditional love. If the child encounters a lack of nurturing energies, it often chooses to relinquish parts of its own identity in order to receive more love. For those born into a loving family, these imprints are stored in the unconscious mind and require awakening in order to release karmic anchors. For those who have chosen and scripted a more challenging family connection, it becomes a prerequisite to awareness. Forgiving our parents therefore, is a vital initial step that will propel us into the evolutionary stepping-stone towards Enlightenment. Overcoming this emotional hurdle reveals the gate out of Duality and frees us from the hooks of abandonment and the illusion of separation.

Once we are able to embrace full acceptance of *forgiveness* within ourselves, the High Mind steps into the higher vibration of Consciousness. This awareness reveals that the word forgiveness does not exist in the Divine Mind. In the Loving God Mind, we, the children are of the highest Light and there is no need for forgiveness within the Divine Family. However, the act of *forgiveness* is a crucial step to take in this human journey. It is not an easy choice and has many implications in the process of transformation. It will be further discussed, expanded and clarified in later chapters.

The next key word is *Surrender.* This word tends to install a fear in the Ego-Mind of having to relinquish its control power. A complete surrender is but the spiritual choice to the acceptance of Divine Presence as the source of our existence. It is a prerequisite to enter the high road of Enlightenment and the first step in weakening the control issues of the Ego. With this choice we gain the wisdom that there is No-thing to be afraid of for we are all held safely within the arms of the Ultimate Loving Divine Parent who looks after our every need. Our needs are met, not our wants and it does not always appear the way we wish according to our limited perceptions of life. We have been given the right of Free Will and our daily choices are the building blocks that create our destiny in Life. It is impossible for the Divine Creator God to create misery and suffering, for the Creator is Light itself and no shadow can exist within the ultimate harmonious vibration of Light and Love.

Once we have completely embraced these words within our understanding, we gain the ability to reinforce them with new strands.

These are the words of Light that become the pass words to open and activate the hidden secret files of elevation into higher states of vibration. The words are stepping stones, or building bricks that create a pathway into the heart and they also provide the Ego-Self with a new behavior mandate. They are different for each person and can be accessed through deep meditation. Meditation is the key state in which the sacred stillness can be reached. For only within the stillness of the Mind can we perceive the spring of knowledge and wisdom. Within this spring we can harvest anything we need for the journey into Enlightenment.

The particles in the Root center are programmed with our unique attributes and qualities accumulated in our past lives. These patterns can be either within the negative or positive ranges of emotions. The Root also hosts the entrance of the Kundalini fire. When activated, the Kundalini's transformative fire rises from the Root Chakra to flame into the prana tube. Flooding the root particles with words of light can be of great assistance in purifying the dark residues and fanning the Kundalini torch into a rising column of light. Continually adding resonating words that carry the intent of manifesting more expansion and cohesion of energies, not only eases the transformations, but ensures the rise and the strength of the Kundalini.

The positive cones contain more light particles and can be used to assist in the cleansing of the negative blocks. Clearing the logjams of negative, fear-based painful emotions within this chakra allows it to spin faster and increase its vibration stimulating the potential of Kundalini awakening. The acquired new higher filaments of awareness will braid together to form a spiralling column of energy that changes into a higher frequency of purplish-red color which emits a more harmonious tone. This column of power forms a stable, grounding foundation into the more powerful new magnetic field within the changing Earth. Imagine building a strong and solid lighthouse upon a huge, stable rock formation.

In its elevated state, the brilliant red color of this center is overlaid with the purplish shade of the purifying Violet Flame. Once the Root has reached the resonating vibrations, it begins to move towards the heart center. The plug, or fuse, is still there, but the energetic color signature is about to join and merge with the Heart Chakra.

The Sacral Chakra

The Second chakra is called the Sacral and it is situated about two inches above the Root. It is connected to the element of Water, has six petals and vibrates with the note D and the color orange. This center deals with all levels of pleasures, not only that of sexual nature, but anything that is pleasing to the human senses, such as reading a good book, enjoying a favorite holiday, fulfilling one's passion and many more. It is the spring of creative thought and the center of the female sexual energies of pro-creation. The blockage here is often mired in the emotions of guilt, low self-esteem, blame, shame and the tattered old blanket of self-loathing that includes acceptance of self-sabotage.

The emotion of guilt is one of the most unnecessary uses of energy and can be released with the acceptance that everything in life is a Soul experience. Accepting and embracing the Shadow-Self and forgiving the self of the illusion of *the badness,* brings the needed peace of mind. Everything in the Universe, including our actions, happen for a reason that most of the time we do not yet comprehend. When we wrap ourselves with guilt and self-flagellation, we are often indulging in the attributes of a child wanting attention. This child-like state loves the drama and it feeds the manipulative parts of the Control-Ego layers.

Using light-filled words here enhances our acceptance that we are all children who are members of one Divine Family. When we infuse this center with positive thought patterns, such as opening ourselves towards the energies of magnetic attraction in order to attract like frequencies, it starts the cleansing flow. There is no blame when we take full responsibility of our choices and grow into the maturity of a spiritual adult. The words from the familiar line, *"Ray, a drop of golden sun"* is very appropriate for this center, as it is sung in the key of D, opening the center and inviting the nourishing golden light of the Great Central Sun of Creation.

The element of water, both physically and etherically, is the healing, purification elixir that washes away the dark and heavy stains in this swirling energy pond. Cleared, this center stimulates, enhances and nourishes the flow of creativity. The color frequency of the Sacral will blend and rise into a sparkling peach hue, hum a higher tone and begin to vibrate in harmony with the Root. Its spiralling and spinning filaments of light joins the current towards the heart.

The Solar Plexus

The Third Chakra is the Solar Plexus, which is situated about two finger-widths above the belly-button and has ten petals. It is connected to the element of Fire, is yellow in shade and spins in the key of E. This center deals with passion and the Will-power of the Soul and it is the stronghold of the Control-Ego-Self. Its roots lie in the belief in the presence of Evil that provides an easy focus for blame.

Lack of understanding and information are the source for the waves of disappointments in our lives. We begin to feel unworthy and left out, as resentment towards others escalates causing us to feed into this trough of low self-esteem. We hunger for love; we seek fulfilment for the craving of wanting. The next line of the song in The Sound of Music helps in facing these dark particles. *"Me. A name I call myself"*, sung in the key of E, brings in the awareness of the Self that encourages the concept of a worthy ME.

We have great fear of what we perceive as Evil. Anger and resentments are the main spices and it burns in the digestive system when we embrace this illusion of unworthiness and the constant attack of evil. It creates the imbalance giving rise to the dis-ease of the endocrine organs of the body situated in the proximity of this center. When we release the child-like demands of *Wanting* and align our passion with Divine Soul-Will, it becomes a commitment and a type of surrender, releasing human expectations of Ego-based outcomes. Asking for the *Most-Benevolent-Outcome (MBO)* clears the road to our destiny and smooth sailing can then be ours.

The Fire element in the Sacral purifies and starts the alchemy of change. The etheric fire, the Kundalini that flows through all the chakras and the prana tube, has the function of burning, purifying and transforming the food of dark emotions into light ashes of healing. When we chose to extinguish the dark fires of fear and anger, it allows the Kundalini fire to take over with its healing properties of alchemy. This transmutation releases the bars that have imprisoned our habitual anger, revengeful resentments and fear-based thoughts of retaliation towards perceived enemies. Healing of physical biology can now proceed.

When we gain clarity, this area will blaze into shining hues of gold. It will be as if the sun is rising above the horizon, heralding a new day accompanied by the sounds of awareness of the ME-Self. For some very energy-sensitive people, it might feel as if one is birthing the sun from a dark womb. The Self can now face its own destiny without fear. The golden rays flow into partnership with the other colors and begin to march gratefully into the heart.

The Throat Chakra

We will by-pass the heart at this point and address the Fifth Chakra, situated in the throat area. This is the center of the Energy of TRUTH. The deep, cobalt blue swirls within this center like stormy clouds and within it, the tones of G can be heard in a painful scream, sobbing remorse or the sweet harmony of the heavens.

It deals with the richness and power of the voice of truth. It is the main line of recognition and communication that affects all our systems. The voice is a powerful tool of creation, for it gave life to the spoken word. The Divine Creator off All Things, the *"I AM"*, gave life to the world when it spoke the words, *"Let there be Light."* When spoken in song, the harmonious vibration of the word rises as it is carried upon the air-waves of musical notes of creative energies. When restricted, the size of this gate is like the eye of a needle that allows only a thin thread to pass. The musical notes of G sung with the words, *"Sow, a needle pulling thread"*, verifies the restrictiveness of the throat when bound, and it often results in the inability to speak out or even to sing.

The Throat Chakra is a very important and vast dimensional gate that provides the power for an instrument, that can broadcast a vast range of frequencies of sound, that can be used for healing, blessings or hurtful harm. This note's remarkable energy has been noted in many legends and spiritual texts in many different societies. It is known generally as the *Interval* of the fifth note and according to the Chinese philosopher Loa Tzu it is the sound of Universal Harmony, balancing the forces of the Ying (Female) and the Yang (Male). In India, this note is believed to create the sound through which Shiva calls Shakti to the dance of Life. In Greek mythology, Apollo the god of Music and Healing plucked the fifth string on his sacred Lyre to call the dolphin messengers to Delphi where they channeled the messages to the Oracles.

The ancient alchemists called it *the Crux Ansata*, considered to be the transition point where matter crossed over into Spirit. The Egyptian scholars called it *Anak,* and assumed it to be the Still Point where the Earth ends and ascension into Spirit begins. For them, the number five carries a sacred energy that represents the unity of Heaven and Earth. The voice, when spoken in alignment with the creative beauty of the heart, allows the Soul to manifest itself into the physical world of men.

This fifth wheel is blocked by fear of speaking one's truth, accepting lies as reality and is frequently wrapped in deceit and the inability to discern the truth. We pollute and restrict the rotation of the wheel with the acceptance of Suffering, therefore closing the door to abundance and the affluence of the Soul. Many accept the chains that imprison the voice when ordered not to be heard. Unfortunately, these chains are often established and imprinted in childhood when the child is bullied with, "*be seen but not heard*".

Suffering creates a lot of drama and becomes the old security blanket. Not only do we relish telling our stories of suffering, but we insist on taking on other people's suffering as well. Inadvertently, we prevent them from learning their life lessons when the Ego-Voice justifies its right to take over the extra baggage. We blatantly assume that it is our duty to rescue others and impose our will upon their lives. Our Ego-Self proclaims to have more experience and to know better, ignoring the protesting voice of the Soul as we force our will onto others. Focussing on others instead of the Self, restrict the flow of our own creativity and keeps it dammed behind the Ego blockage.

The voice of gossip is another powerful current in the dark stream of suffering. The human language is a versatile tool and can be used as a weapon to hurt or a soothing balm to heal. Thoughts are carried through the voice that speaks the words that can manifest it into reality. When we target and limit our words to those of negative shadows of criticism and judgments, we create boundaries, walls and bars within our reality. The walls and bars are reflective mirrors that project our own imbalances in our lives. A sage once said, "*When you name it you claim it*".

When speech is allowed to be heard freely, it allows freedom from past restrictions and opens the gate for the creative abundance to enter. Recognition of the difference between the heavier and lighter vibrations of the energetic strands of words tends to open this gate more towards the understanding of karmic relationships. By accepting ourselves the way we are and speaking our truth without trying to hide behind lies of who we are NOT, we learn to make the right choices. When we allow our true nature to flow with the spoken words and enhance them with compassion and respect, we break through the tight bonds that have imprisoned our voices. By choosing to use the words of Light instead of lies and un-truth, we release the dam of silent suffering.

When we balance this Chakra, we allow the healing energies to alleviate the suffering of depression and hopelessness and begin the balancing of many internal organs, such as the heart, the pituitary gland and the nervous systems. It encourages the expansion of lung capacity for increased oxygen intake, thus relaxing the throat and chest muscles. Released from its Ego-shackles, the Throat Chakra is freed to explode into crashing waves of blues, at times overlaid with filaments of violet. These variations may include cobalt blue, sky blue and ice-blue which expand the vocal cords and enriches the voice with the ability to speak the higher vibrational tones of universal truth. A voice that has not been allowed to speak may suddenly sing and soar into the heavens, as the releasing energies of peace and joy flood the mind. Developing the conscious sacred breath of life effortlessly enhances and strengthens the channels towards the sacred heart center.

These higher frequencies of sound begin to spiral into the heart and join the three other strands, initiating the creation of a new heart-song. This song will permeate and pulse from the heart, rising into Soul-song flowing into the blood stream and bring alchemy of harmonious cohesion to the molecular structure of the body. It is the awareness of the presence of the harmonic essence that is the translation of light frequency into sound.

The Third Eye Chakra

From the Throat Chakra, we move into the Third Eye Chakra located between the brows on the forehead. It is the center for the Inner Sight that we recognize as the psychic sight and the connecting line to the higher senses. It pulses in the range of the Indigo color and resonates in the note of A. The words sung in the following line, *"La, a note to follow sow"*, is the opening note to activate the Third Eye center. This Chakra can only function fully when supported by the complete opening of the Throat Chakra. Thus it follows the musical bars of the fifth Interval.

The Third Eye Chakra is blocked by a belief in illusions of separation of all things. It is the non-acceptance of Oneness and the Integration with the Divine Creator Energy that is present in the Universe. A veil is created over this area when we are unwilling to *see* the truth beyond the illusions of Duality. The veil thickens and completely blinds the inner sight, when the Ego of Will and Vanity is allowed to occupy this center. As a result, a type of tunnel vision dominates our sight and narrows our awareness of the greater realms of existence. The firm hold of the Ego here affects our state of mind, firmly anchoring it into the Duality box influencing our daily decision making based on the choice of Free Will.

Once we recognize our limitations and realize that there are no boundaries, we can do and experience anything we wish in this world. The etheric veils will be drawn back, layer after layer. The Inner sight opens and the veils lift, as we accept the ultimate knowingness of Oneness. Every cell and every atom in our bodies is also found in everything around us including the stars and the moon. Embracing this Oneness will allow us to see that a diamond is but a piece of petrified wood chunk that was transformed through the process of alchemy. The same carbon particles flow in our biology as well. The, "*I AM THAT, I AM* "becomes part of the Soul's awareness and raises the level of our Consciousness as human beings. We begin to look at our world in a different light. We reach the wisdom that the word THAT embraces the revealing fact that we are part of and one with, everything around us including the rocks, the flowers, the mouse in the garden and the neighbor next door.

The indigo strands become a vibrant flow of violet filaments and accompanied by the higher notes, it too begins to connect with the heart.

The Crown Chakra

Next, we reach the top of the head where the Crown Chakra is anchored. It radiates in violet shades and sings to B. It is the connection to the Pure Cosmic energies that have an endless flow to our Over-Soul. The Over-Soul is the direct link to the Divine I AM that clarifies infinity. The I AM is forever and cannot be unmade and we are all part of it. There is no DEATH for the eternal Spirits that we are, for we are the immortal Soul part of the human-Soul symbiotic partnership. This center is the ultimate gate to our Divine Source within the higher realms of Consciousness and provides the clarity of inter-dimensionality of Being. Embracing this center gives us a sense of Sacredness, a sense of something Holy and when fully integrated, it fills us with the joy of coming Home. The words sung in the B frequency, *"Ti, a drink with jam and bread"*, are the invitation to the celebration party when we enter the halls of the Over-Soul.

The denial or refusal, to acknowledge the presence of the Christ Consciousness within the Self locks this gate tightly. The blockage causes great reluctance to face our own existence as Soul-Spirit Beings. When we label ourselves and insist on the statement "I am only human," we create a boundary with the Ego-sense of unworthiness. It becomes a containment field, a box with a beginning, middle and an ending. We built the walls with our belief that physical death is final, that our essence is completely obliterated and that there is no after-life.

When we declare to the world, **I AM**, we acknowledge our heritage as immortal Beings and are released from the imprisonment of the box. A complete surrender to the Divine Light Consciousness opens this Chakra fully and allows the energy of the sensations of inifinity and immortality to flow freely into the mind. To emphasize again, surrender does not mean that we lose our identity, it only means that we choose to detach from the earthly attachments. We begin to break free from the brainwashing of the belief that material wealth is the ultimate reality in human life and that we are separate entities living in a separate universe. Detaching from relationships does not mean that we do not love any less. It is actually the other way around. Our deeper understanding of Divine Unconditional Love allows us to let our loved ones go, to experience and reach their own potential. Complete surrender to the Higher-Soul-Self and stepping onto non-duality deepens and strengthens the Love quotient that is necessary to open this gate into the path to enlightenment.

The Crown Chakra is thought to vibrate with a thousand petals. The petals are the rotating cones anchored in the Pineal gland that form into a funnel, opening to the connecting channel to Soul-Source. When cleared of all debris, all the cones or petals of the funnel radiate with a pulsing pearlescent white beam emitting the high notes of harmony. This higher beam loops into the heart to be connected, intertwined and braided with the other six beams, creating a powerful column of light that will rise to the heavens. For those with the gift of clairvoyant sight, it will appear as if a constellation of stars, a shining galaxy is swirling in and around the Crown.

The Heart Chakra

From the top of the head we return our gaze to the chest, where the heart is located. Within the old structure, the Heart Chakra spins with twelve cone-shaped petals in a sea of emerald green, resonating to F. Each cone contains 12 crystal particles and at the base of each cone lies the large water crystal, which is the Love crystal of the Heart. The large diamond-shaped crystal pulsates with the pink divine love energy and is frequently depicted as containing a blooming pink rose.

The water crystals are the anchoring points of the Love-body and form an interface structure between the Love-body and the Light-body. Most of us are not aware that the human Heart Chakra carries many of the original wounds and trauma of the initial times of separation from the ultimate source of Unity Consciousness. To release these ancient congestions, a cleansing current has to be channelled through the love-lines that contain the Love water crystals. The water element, therefore is taking the lead here, for it provides the water-love-lines through which the water crystals flow from each cone, connecting the love energies to the galactic, universal and cosmic strata.

The Heart Chakra has always been associated with the energy of human Love and Compassion. It is the most vital organ, for it is a direct line to our main source of Unconditional Divine Love which is the energy of Light and the receptacle of Life as we know it. It is the sacred vault where the Christ Seed of Light is kept in safety, within a higher dimensional reality. The Heart is structured as an unlimited conduit to the Source of Love and its function is to oversee the process that transforms the dark particles of emotions into light particles of Unconditional Love. It is the ultimate laboratory of alchemy. It is the main entrance conduit through which flows the powerful Love-Light particles to support manifestation of creation in the physical realms.

The biggest obstruction is the misunderstanding of the energy of LOVE. We assume that it is an act of love when we try to control others or subjugate others to our Ego-Will. A blockage is formed when we mire ourselves in the emotions of grief and self-denial and accept pain as a means of punishing ourselves for feelings of guilt. The Ego of the lower mind often chooses to wallow in self-pity and enjoys the victim-hood dramas involved. We accept the illusion that self-love is an act of selfishness and deny our right to self-fulfilment. Today's media, which depicts so-called Hollywood love scenes, tends to infiltrate all our senses and the true meaning of the word LOVE is lost in the frenzy to fill our yearning to be loved. We equate Ego-control actions as acts of love when we demand that we have the solutions to everyone else's problems and take part in the dramas involved. These major congestions eventually manifest in a variety of dis-eases in the organs and the physical heart. When we ignore the clues and signs of imbalance in the lower bodies, it creates blockage in the crystal-love-lines and results in disharmony within the heart-water-crystal. To release these strong emotions of un-love, we must choose to face them and accept the truth that we are part of a Greater Reality of Eternal Oneness. It is imperative that we open the mind and accept the fact that we carry the sacred God-gene, the God DNA, within us. When we do not direct the love to our inner God-Self first we lack the wisdom of clarity and are not capable of truly loving another being. The love we proclaim to have for another person is but a poor reflection, an imitation, for it is mired in layers of conditions and the small prints of expectations.

Every emotional attachment and every choice is experienced and held, in the fibres of the heart. It is a record of how well we have learned the lessons of Divine Love. Clearing the Heart-Core is one of the most difficult challenges for the human partner and the words sung in the tones of F remind us of this journey with, *"Fa, a long, long way to run"*. The road to enlightenment is a long road and requires courage, determination and complete commitment for all seekers who choose to travel on it.

When we finally accept our own limitations and release the painful memories through the light-filled words of forgiveness and surrender, we open the doors for the energy of Divine love to heal us. Healing begins when we enter the stillness within the sacred chamber of the Heart and fill our chalice with love of self, with the understanding that it is not an act of selfishness. The healing of the self has to happen first, before we can begin to offer our assistance to anyone else. The overflow of the cup of love within the Heart center will never be depleted when fully connected to the Divine Source within. It is the only elixir that can successfully be shared with other, for how can anyone claim to love another when the heart is empty, or half full of the Love Energy of the Self? How can we help someone else when the Self is ill and incapacitated?

The changes are more pronounced as we surrender to the metamorphoses and allow the transformational process to take its next step. Human tears are the sacred raindrops that fall freely into the Heart when we enter and accept the higher frequencies of consciousness. The healing waters of tears will wash away the ashes and the debris of pain, bringing peace into the heart. This sacred rain begins to nourish the green meadow of the Heart and awaken the seed of the rose. A beautiful, etheric pink bud first appears within the large water-crystal of the Heart center and with encouragement from the still mind, blossoms into a vibrant pink rose, the symbol of love. The rose petals will grow larger as the sacred chalice of Love begins its overflow and it takes over most of the green meadow. A sage once said that *tears are liquid prayers of the soul that are offered upon the altar of Divine Unconditional Love.*

As the Heart Chakra opens itself to the flow of all the other Chakras, the energetic sounds of harmony, joy and laughter permeates and surrounds the whole system, raising the vibrational frequency of the power lines. The Heart eventually restructures into a highly advanced technical control center. It becomes the new Root Chakra, the new solar-power center and the grounding base for the new human construct. This new center is the Zero-Still-Point area and has the capability to store our increased cosmic energy particles. It allows us free access to an infinite amount of crystalline particles to use and to share with others. However to maintain balance, we can only integrate the amount that resonates with our present level of awareness and the access is to be circulated as a constantly moving current of quantum cosmic energy.

The new Root is anchored within the higher vibrations and begins to feed the *Tree of life* with the elixirs of the Ethers, the fifth element. It is the long awaited chance for the entrance of the fifth element to take its place and join the residing four Earth elements. As noted earlier, the individual six Chakra anchors are still there, but their energetic signatures have merged within the Heart and form a center of power that will provide the energies needed for the rebuilding process.

Healing of the system continues after the initial breakthroughs and is in direct correlation to the individual's spiritual growth and awareness. Each rising step towards the higher calibrations promotes the increase in the energetic flow and its vibrating waves are transported, and directed to every physical and etheric layer of the human structure through the new Root. The higher frequency of the energy flow releases the restrictions of the opposing forces of Duality allowing us to travel with less effort.

CHAPTER FOUR

The Merkabah Vehicle

It was noted earlier that to ensure further protection for the Soul against the fluctuations of interdimensional space the human vessel is encapsulated within an energetic *spacesuit*. It cocoons the energetic golden, egg shaped capsule within layers of an intricate geometric pattern called the Merkabah. In the ancient tongue, the syllable Mer means Light; Ka refers to the Spirit; and Bah refers to the body. In the Hebrew language, Merkabah translates as *the vehicle or chariot of the Gods*. Based upon its structure, the Merkabah is perceived as a rotating, spiralling, field of light particles that form the basic model of the light-body vehicle. This vehicle has many parts of what is considered sacred geometric shapes in the form of pyramids of multiple facets. The pyramids are counter rotating prisms interconnected to the chakra system which correlate to the energies of the elements. Within dimensional space, all sections are interconnected with a vast communication network run by the twelve DNA com-link. The following is a quick overview of their energetic functions.

The hexahedron, a cube based prism, is connected to the Earth Element and associated with the Root Chakra. It deals with anchoring and grounding energies into the Earth's magnetic grid. It has six faces, each with four sides, eight vertices and twelve edges. It carries the energy of **Divine Creativity**.

The Icosahedron works with the element of Water and is connected to the Sacral Chakra. This shape deals with changes, as in '*going with the flow*' and has the capability of removing and flushing out emotional blockages. It projects the energies of **Divine Wisdom**. This prism rotates with twenty faces each with three sides, twelve vertices and thirty edges.

The Tetrahedron is powered by the element of Fire and focusses on the Solar Plexus Chakra. Here lies the personal power of acceptance and the force of the Will. It has four equilateral triangular faces, each with three sides, four vertices and six edges. This shape rotates in sync with a descending male and ascending female part. It is identified as the Star of David, a symbol adopted by the Jewish tradition, as a statement of their believe system. This shape is of utmost importance for it is present in the molecular foundation particles of creation. It represents **Divine Will.**

The *Octahedron* is connected to the element of Air and linked to the Heart Chakra. This eight—faced structure, each with three sides, six vertices and twelve edges, looks at the transformational words of forgiveness, compassion and Love. It promotes **Divine Unity** of all things.

The *Dodecahedron* is tied to the fifth element, the Ethers and it envelops the three upper body centers, which include the Third Eye Chakra, the Crown and the Souls Star Chakra. This twelve faced pyramid, each with five sides, twenty vertices and thirty edges represents the expression of life and consciousness. It is the connecting link to the Higher-self and Creative Divine Source, enveloped within the energy of **Divine Compassion**. Note that divine compassion is not to be confused with human Compassion, for it deals with two very different energies. This sacred, geometric shape is the corridor or pathway to go beyond the physical body and reconnect with the true spirit-self, the Over-Soul.

The whole structure, at the same time is connected and linked by circular, energetic shapes. Within each circle are intricately woven, intersecting, energy lines that form the pattern of the petals of a flower and it is therefore, identified as *the flower of life*. The center of each flower is termed a node and the pattern is tied and linked into a cube formation called Metatron's Cube. These rotating energy fields are immediately activated as soon as the Soul begins its entry into density and merges with its human host.

As we begin to move faster into the Great Shift of Consciousness, the recalibration and rebuilding continue to occur simultaneously everywhere. Every strand within the grid of the matrix is on the move. The triggering points begin within the etheric filaments, because they are the finest, gossamer-like fibers that vibrate at a higher speed than the heavier strands of biology. This is one reason why the chakra panels needed to be recalibrated first. As the rotation of the chakra wheels begin to accelerate into a faster spin it activates the resonating **points** in the Merkabah and they begin to pulse and broadcast energetic waves at a higher rate.

This acceleration sequence in turn, oozes down into the slower moving matter of biology. To achieve this extraordinary move a tremendous amount of energy is needed. Prior to this point, the human construct was running on electrical energies that were operated and influenced by the dominant male strands of energy. To reach the higher frequencies, we must recalibrate to a magnetic vibration that contain more feminine components, creating a balanced conduit.

When the human prototype was created, it was powered with the appropriate electrical currents through conductors of water and carbon molecules. In order to increase the light quotient, the conductors had to be changed. The carbon molecules were not be able to withstand the higher electrical charges needed and therefore, had to be transfigured to a silicon based molecule that has the capability to work with stronger magnetic frequencies. The stronger and bigger the magnet, the more electrical power we can harvest for our homes. In the same manner increasing the magnetic qualities from within our core center causes more production of energetic power that accelerates the engines of the *human space-capsule*.

The Merkabah is a type of a Soul-Human space-shuttle and it is has the capability of transporting the spirit-body from one dimension into another. Its known system up to this point is attuned to gendered polarity dominated by the male energies within the tetrahedron. At this imbalanced level, it is incapable of sustaining the acceleration of tremendous speed required for a *lift-off boost*. Imagine an electrical wire that can only carry a low sixty watt current that is subjected, or plugged into the main power source that emits one thousand watts of power. The end result of incineration of the lower wire is of course, a predictable outcome.

The start button to activate the transfiguration is located deep within a small sacred compartment in the Heart-Core, and when pushed it will have a domino-like effect that cannot be stopped. Once triggered within the new, recalibrated Heart center, the panel begins to hum with increased power, producing more light radiance. The enhanced light particles begin to flow and spiral as fibre optic filaments into the tetrahedron, stimulating it into a crystalline configuration. It is flooded with the frequencies of united, crystalline-bonded light particles and begins to emit stronger light beams. The tetrahedron symbolizes the energies of Divine Will and when we surrender to it, the Star-of-David transitions into a non-gendered, balanced and non-polar energetic shape. This new shape begins to rotate uniformly in a faster spin, producing a pulsing burst of brilliant crystal light. This new configuration has been coined as the *Merkiva* and becomes the core for the new *spaceship-spacesuit*.

The increasing speed of Light of the Merkiva in turn activates the cube-like Hexahedron, transforming the structure further into the Merkava. The light quotient flares intensify even higher and further energizes the next star, the Icosahedron, shape-shifting it into the Merkana. Meanwhile, the Octahedron, the heart center, continually monitors all changes within the layered structure. If this speed is maintained, and the acceleration continues without any interruptions, the configurational structure of this sacred geometry then morphs into the final stages of the new space-suit. Like a newborn sun, it explodes into the star Dodecahedron that blazes into the Merkara, the ascended Lightbody. The word, 'spin' is an inadequate description for this spectacular vision, for it pulses, spirals, dances and radiates with living light essences. A new living star is born.

New names or labels are periodically added to the human vocabulary in order to promote deeper understanding of the Shift and the nature of the strands of creation. It is but a pebble in the stream of ultimate Consciousness and free access to its files is available to any seeker of knowledge. Naming things is a human impulse, for labeling it creates a boundary or limitation, on the path directed by Duality. Claiming it strengthens the walls of this boundary of unrealized human potentiality and it allows the Ego another peek around the corner. The names we have utilized and are using at the moment are for our human benefit to give us the comfort and familiarity we need. It will be kept in play until we step out of Duality completely and embrace the higher Consciousness of neutrality, which is the stepping stone, or bridge to Ultimate Oneness acceptance.

For those who have achieved this metamorphosis, a star-constellation-like apparition can be sensed by those with advanced inner sight. It would be as if a new universe is spiralling around the person enhancing the stream of star-light that is already flowing out from the Heart through the Crown. The speed of the rotation of the one thousand petals of the original Crown Chakra will have formed the funnel-like stream, wherein a new galaxy of stars can be detected.

However, it must be noted that this recalibration cannot happen upon a separate track. As discussed before, everything is interlinked and inter-connected like a chain link or a weave of a spider web. The new power grid has to be strung and anchored within a resonating, accepting field before the ultimate light-switch can be turned on.

The current to supply the transformation of the sacred geometric vessel has to be channelled via the chakra panel and directed from the Heart core through the biology of the brain. The bioelectric fluctuations coursing through the brain synapses and the nervous system operate from a dualistic template. There are many junction points in the brain that have been kept dormant until the human vessel is ready to remodel this template. Throughout our Duality-based life-times, we have accumulated numerous heavy thought-patterns in the brain. This has influenced our decision-making and polluted our mental and emotional bodies. This heavy debris has knotted the links, causing a type of sluggishness within the Chakra board which prevents a clear flow of energy throughout the system of the human construct. All connecting lines must be cleared before the final switch can be activated.

There are about four main Gama brainwave activities that sustain and maintain the human level of consciousness. The most accepted level is the Beta wave. It vibrates at the junction of the neck, and the head and pulses through the Medulla Oblongata. This is an entry point located at the center of the back of the head that forms the beginning part of the brain stem. The current flows through the etheric spinal cord that we know as the prana tube. It is connected to the chakra system. The quality and speed of the current traveling along this highway determines the brainwave pattern. It resembles the staff of a shepherd, with the crook at the top, as the Golden Spiral curl inside the brain. When the tube-like staff enters the Medulla Oblongata, it begins to curve into a tight curl that ends in the Pineal gland, deep in the center of the brain. The curve follows the mathematical formula of the *Fibonacci spiral*, also called the *Golden Ratio*. This pattern of creation is found all around us, such as the curve in a shell or the pattern of the petals of a flower. This awakening knowledge gives us the awareness that everything created within our perception is based on mathematical formulas that are still beyond our human intelligence. The very presence of the same Golden Ratio we carry and is found in all living entities around us, can only substantiate the fact that we are all connected within a web of Creative Oneness.

The Beta wave is a natural basic rhythm of the presence of the five senses and pulses at the entrance of the brain stem. It is an unconscious awareness that recognizes the boundaries of time and space in which we live. This wave accommodates the thoughts of anxiety and worry, relating it to the appropriate chakra center. Most humans who chose not to walk the road of Spirituality embrace this level quite comfortably. It is often identified as the point of Initiation for we have initial awareness of other realities and have the opportunity to begin to ask more questions. We might even feel the need to begin our search for spiritual guidance when we allow this wave to evolve out of its comfort zone.

From the Beta area, the energy flows into the curve along the cortex of the brain and vibrates in the Alpha wave when stimulated. This can be experienced in a light, sleep-state awareness when we begin to reach a deeper meditative level where there is no time and space. It is similar to being in a dream-like reality. Here we reach the ability to connect to the Spiritual Triad of, the Will, Intuition and the High Mind. It is identified as the state of Communion for we begin to become aware of the Spiritual world and begin communication with the Inner levels of Consciousness. Extra Sensory Perceptions (ESP) and expanded thought patterns may occur in this beginning altered state. There is a great potential for us to be unprepared for entrance into this level when we experience a sudden spiritual awakening. It can be a traumatic experience if we face it without guidance from a knowledgeable and capable counselor or spiritual healer.

New synapses in the brain are connected as the Alpha waves begin to flow in the current along the Golden Spiral. The energetic current that increases in frequency initiates a higher vibration that pulses along all the filaments within the energy grid that connects all the systems. It flows into, and out of the prana tube, stimulating and energizing the chakra junctions within the heart. It triggers a resonating vibration that radiates into the Merkabah structure. Increasing and intensifying the Alpha wave through deeper meditation, awakens the faster Theta brain wave pattern when we choose to walk the path of the spiritual seeker.

Theta vibration pulses along the stretch in the approximation of the Pituitary gland that oversees the Third Eye gate. This brainwave vibration heralds the entrance into mastery and ascension. This is a deep-sleep pattern of relaxation while the mind remains alert, active and aware. It delves deeply into the realms of the High-Mind. Decades ago, this level was only accessible by the monks, gurus and shamans, but with the entrance of the new energies, this level is now within reach for all of us.

This frequency enhances the speed of the fiber-optic light filaments even more, throwing the points of the pyramidal prisms of the Merkabah layers into greater spins, thus raising the brilliance of the emanations of light rays. It is the beginning of the manifestation of the Light-body vehicle preparing it for the Delta frequencies. It is the alarm clock to awaken the Soul parts out of their dream state into a more heightened connection to their human counterparts.

The spiral ends in its final tight curl within the centre of the Pineal Gland. This is the sanctuary of the Delta brainwave pattern of a deep, dreamless, sleep pattern with total awareness in the High Mind. The Soul begins to stir out of its slumber and becomes aware of a loss of density connectedness and a sensation of being bodiless, that in turn leads to a sensation of euphoric bliss. Approaching this level heralds the beginning of the awareness of non-duality and the brain steps into a higher trance-state of Consciousness. The platform of non-duality brain waves exists outside of the dualistic matrix of the nervous system, and communication with the higher vibrational realities can now proceed. Reaching this station stimulates the high platform of the Merkabah, which is the Merkara configuration that initiates the ability to navigate the multi-dimensional highways. This is the realm of the ascended Masters who are entering the higher dimensional vibrations, after releasing all ties to the human personality and immersed themselves into the energies of non-duality. This is a high place of functioning and it enables the Master to ascend into the realms of Light Consciousness where the Over-Soul resides. The enlightened Master has obtained the capability to travel all the etheric pathways and gain complete access to the river of Divine Unity knowledge.

For a long time, only a small group of ascended Masters, such as Jesus, have been able to reach this level of enlightenment. The birth of the Great Shift has reversed this trend opening the doors for anyone who wishes to walk this road. The price is still steep, for it requires full payment from the Soul-human traveler. The method of payment of course is complete surrender to the Light-Self by releasing the *Little-i-ego-self* and detaching from the chains of Duality. It is not an easy path to travel, but it is an obtainable destination for any courageous, brave and determined Soul-human who is ready to lift all anchors and detach from the three dimensional harbor. For those who continue to work on recalibrating themselves with a strong determination of purpose, the question becomes, *"Are you ready to step in and ride the blazing Chariot of the Gods?"*

CHAPTER FIVE

The Communication Network

In order to keep all departments informed and working in sync, a vast communication system has to be in place and this has been the job of the DNA-helix components. Within the range of Duality, only the double-helix DNA strand is visible and acceptable as part of human biology. In reality, there are twelve strands with more than two helix spirals that were already wired into the human matrix. It was kept dormant and waiting within the etheric, dimensional folds until the vibrational conditions were compatible. When the new agreement came into play, this extensive network was activated and put in working order.

Our scientists know that the spirals of the double helix rotate around geometric configurations we recognize as part of the Merkabah structure. They suspect that there is more than what they are able to detect and are diligently probing deeper into the DNA puzzle. The information they seek has been gifted to us through a number of channels, and the Goddess has included this present information to help us gain more knowledge and clarity.

The first three layers are deemed to be the Grounding, foundation layers and are followed by the next three Human Divine sequences. Numbers seven, eight and nine deal with our Lemurian experiences; acquired knowledge of healing and awareness of connected Oneness within interdimensionality. The last three sections are in a different category for they connect the system to the *super-long-distance* high speed communication channels of the Divine God layers. In human terms, the DNA network is similar to that of the intricate, wireless communication grid that we, in the twenty-first century, are familiar with. The big difference is that DNA lines do not function on linear sequential lines, for they connect our biology centers to the higher dimensional lines of Soul-Spirit communication. Their attribute is that when one line is blocked, all the others will react and respond in sync and put all requests for activation on hold. We received them in a numbered list, but their number allotments are there to meet our human knowledge of linear numerical values. Their names are noted in the Hebrew language, an ancient tongue that is considered to carry a high vibrational frequency of sound. In order to activate the system, we need to study and gain deeper understanding of each layer's function and connection to the dimensional network. *No one* can activate anyone else's DNA system, for each is fully responsible and accountable for the work involved and the type of structure that is chosen. It is the persuasive voice of the Ego-persona that presents the illusion that we have the power to activate someone else's system.

DNA 1—Keter Etz Chayim—Biological Layer

This is the foundation layer, the grounding section and it is the line connecting all biology parts to the Earth's communication grid. It is perceived as *the Tree of Life* that roots and grounds into the Earth like a massive tree of light. Its center is the heart, where the seed of light has awakened into germination and grown into a semblance of a tree. The heart energy, combined with the four elements of Earth essences is the nourishing elixir that feeds the tree and keeps it healthy. When full grown, the tree trunk becomes the main prana channel connecting the chakra system to all internal organs.

However, when there are numerous heavy blockages churning in the chakra wheels especially the Root Chakra, this DNA spiral has difficulty maintaining its connecting links. The Tree-of-Life cannot grow to its full potential, because it has not received the amount of nourishments it needs. The elixir has to use a lot of energy to find ways to flow past the obstacles formed by the dark emotional debris that has not been cleared, and the messages cannot be sent, nor received with clarity. The Tree-of-Life blooms into the new enlightened tree when the water crystal in the heart core has been awakened and the energy of the ethers have begun to nourish the tree.

DNA 9—Shechinah Esh—Lemurian Healing Layer

Number nine supports number one and allows the purifying energy of
the Violet Flame to flow and clear any blockages along the channels.
The Violet Flame is the etheric fire that can be invoked through
meditation and intent, for it is the only fire that is able to annul, purify
and transmute dark energies. This DNA spiral connects to the Lemurian
records of healing modalities and accesses that knowledge in order to
allow the expansion of consciousness in the cellular cores within the
Tree of Life. This line forms the bridge from healing into the step of
Mastery that flows into the activation of communication lines towards
enlightenment. The Lemurian records are those kept in the Akash, and
they are the accumulated knowledge the Soul-human gained during
the time of life in the Lemurian Age of existence. During their Earthen
life-times, the Lemurians were more aware of the connection to Oneness
with the divine God Light frequency and had gained much wisdom. In
Hebrew, the word Shekinah is another name for Divine God. The word
Shekinah has also been found in many ancient belief systems where it
translates as the Ultimate Divine Mother presence. According to legend,
She appeared as a brilliant female form surrounded by lightening beams
of pulsing Light. To the ancient tribes, this apparition looked like a
Spider-Woman-Goddess. To this day there are societies where the spider
is considered a very sacred animal and its presence looked upon as a
blessing of the Holy Mother Goddess. When activated, this powerful line
accelerates the energetic flow of consciousness expansion into the cellular
structure, opening communication lines to the higher aphelion.

DNA 2—Torah E'ser Spirot—Life Lesson Blueprint Layer

The second grounding layer shows the blueprint of our life-lesson
history. Everything that has not been learned or karmically cleared is
recorded and added or deleted from the blueprint. This line provides an
opportunity for us to look at the word *lesson*. Only the human vessel is
faced with lessons in accordance with the requirements of Duality. There
are no lessons to be learned for the Soul partner for it is a member of
the family of All-That-Is, the source of all knowledge and wisdom. For
the Soul it is a record of experiences to be included in the Blueprint of
wisdom. When This DNA spiral is cleared and activated, the revised

blueprint becomes the grounding template, a vital part of the new foundation. Updated records and instructions can then be relayed to the cellular restructuring teams.

DNA 8—Rochev Baara Vot—Lemurian Wisdom and Responsibility Layer

This is a second Lemurian section in support of layer number two. The communicating spiral lines carry the accumulated results of human lessons learned. It harvests and records the Wisdom and Acceptance of Responsibility that have been achieved by the human and sends them to be used in the redrawing of the blueprint. This DNA chain is in charge of monitoring the Master Records. It receives the information from line number two and stores all changes and adaptations in the Master Files in the Akashic Hall of Records. Number eight spirals into number nine, Shechinah Esh, enabling greater expansion of consciousness in direct correlation to the changes within the Master ledgers.

DNA 3—Netzach Merkava Eliyahu— Grounding Ascension Activation layer

The third grounding layer is a strand that grounds the Tree of Life deeper into the Divine Planet. It carries the message that our lives are intricately connected to the Earth's vibration. It reminds us that we are part of the pattern of evolution of the whole. As we heal ourselves, so does the planet and vice versa. We jeopardize this connection when we deny or devalue the Earth's richness with pollutions within the density of the elements and the etheric layers of emotional thought patters. The root of the Tree of Life when fully intertwined within the energetic web of the Divine Planet, will enhance and strengthen our interdimensional pathways towards full potentiality.

DNA number 6—Eyeh Asher Eyeh—I AM THAT I AM—Higher-Self Communication Layer

Number three is supported and energized by number six with the powerful mantra of *I AM THAT I AM*. When we recognize the presence of our higher-selves by meaningfully stating I Am That I Am, we open the files of our Human Divine records. The word **THAT** awakens us to the reality that we are all connected and that each choice we make has an impact on everything in our lives.

The following scenarios are droplets of examples for us to examine. Everything on this Earth was created for us to use as a support mechanism in our quest towards enlightenment. For example, we need wood to build our homes, furniture, and other usable items. For centuries we have blatantly cut our forests down to harvest this seemingly unlimited resource. What we have not realized is that the living essence within the tree is also flowing within us and that there is awareness in all living substances. A very psychically sensitive person has the ability to '*hear*' a tree *scream* as it is being cut. There is trauma energy in the wood that is logged and carried through into the boards. When we accept the fact that the tree is in the word THAT followed by I AM, we see that we are in oneness with the tree. The peoples who are in oneness with the forest understand that when we communicate with the tree and ask its permission for the use of its *body parts,* then we gain an energetically vibrant supporting product. The tree gives willingly, for it knows that it is created for human support. It withdraws its living essence back into the Earth and thus will not suffer the wrenching, separating and violent action of the saw. The ancient sages knew that anything made from such a compassionate and respectful harvest contain a very strong energy of loving support from Mother Nature. Artistic renditions made from this harvest end up as sacred artefacts because of the energetic powers they contain.

The same theory applies to anything we harvest for our consumption. A number of societies have already adapted their practices of acknowledging the life essences of anything harvested especially our meat source. The energies of fear, pain and suffering are felt by animals in the same manner that a human faces termination through physical death. This dark, emotional energy of trauma is lodged within the cellular structure of the meat harvested without acknowledgement, respect and thanksgiving. When we consume this food source, we ingest the heavy energies attached to it, causing our cells to deal with all the additional congestion of dark energy, and building more blockages in the process. Fully embracing and accepting I AM—THAT (tree, water, animal etc.)—I AM, ignites this DNA spiral into open communication with the Higher-Over-Soul-Self. It opens the gate, enabling Divine messages to flow freely into the network. In addition, it activates the ascending link to the third Grounding branch that establishes and connects to the Earth's *'long distance line'*. We send the message to Mother Nature that we respect her living essence and are grateful for the nourishments she is providing for us.

DNA number 4—Urim Ve Tunim—Human Divine Layer of Core Crystal Energy

This is the Divine wiring connection within the human structure. There is a dormant Crystal Energy Core within our structure and the password to open this file is the sacred Angelic name that the Soul chooses when it enters biology. Opening this file allows the Soul to remember and recognize its identity signature of being a true Divine Self. The veil of memory is lifted and the Soul further acknowledges the connection of the Self to Gaia, the Living Divine Planet. This branch follows number three, the ascension activation section. The Soul awakens when it hears its angelic code name and helps the human partner to make the choice of walking the ascending pathway within Earth's reality.

DNA number 5—Aleph Etz Adonai— Human Divine Essence of Life Layer

Number five is closely related and works together with number four. Here the Soul component accepts the Angelic name and begins to tap into the Core Crystal Energy of the Self. This is the link to the Essence of Life that runs through the veins of the Tree of Life. This line is strengthened with the mantra of number six, I AM THAT I AM. Both numbers four and five open the broadcasting station that sends the message of our understanding and acceptance of Oneness with the planet. The Earth Mother accepts the transmission joyfully for she has been waiting for the opening of this line for a very long time.

DNA number 7—Kadumah Elohim— Lemurian Revealed Divinity Layer

Once more we tap into the Lemurian library of knowledge. This record reveals to us that we are wired with an extra-dimensional awareness and an awakening to the sense of who we truly are. We begin to acknowledge with more ease that we are members of an extensive Divine Family, and that we are on a journey of discovery with our brothers and sisters. One layer of the blinding veils of forgetfulness is torn away as we enter this level. This awareness is enhanced by number eight as we tap into the communication links of the Master Akashic records. Number nine comes into play once again as the bridge, the encouraging, nurturing and compassionate Mother presence, that assists in accelerating the process of ascension, healing and mastery of the Divine-Self.

DNA numbers 8 and 9 could be repeated after number 7, if one wishes to follow the sequential number line.

DNA number 10—Va Yik Ra—The Call to Recognition of the Divinity Within

Number ten heralds the activation of the first Divine-God layer of the Communication Network. This is an active, action station that begins to broadcast the call to Divinity. It rings with the message that there is a direct link to our Divine Source of Existence and prods us to accept our unlimited membership to this line. The High-Mind opens the curtains and the blinds, showing us that the Divine-God-energy has always been inside of us. We are the Divine Godlings, and there truly is no need for intermediary assistance to communicate with our parent Divine source. This Divine-long-distance-line is free and infinitely accessible to everyone.

DNA number 11—Chochmah Micha Halelu— The Divine Feminine Compassion Layer

This second God-layer is an extension line that is a direct link connecting us to the Divine Feminine. It allows direct communication with the Divine Mother Creator, the sacred and holy energy, that embraces us with wisdom and lovingly nurtures us infinitely. This strand prods us to tap into our human centers of inner wisdom of compassion. Human Compassion works within the framework of three dimensional duality and is the first step towards the ladder of evolution. This emotion evokes the Duality thought patterns that something is wrong and needs our help. When we act upon these feelings of compassion and forgiveness towards others, we experience the emotions of satisfaction, relief and a sense that we have contributed to the welfare of our human family. Climbing up the next rung of the ladder, we are faced with the idea of detached compassion. From this platform we still acknowledge that there is something wrong but we have gained the wisdom of not stepping into and taking part of the drama involved with the situation. For example, we might wish to assist those in need with a monetary donation, but at the same time we detach and remove ourselves from the emotion of expectation and from the drama. We do not feel the need to get involved any longer, or even to expect any kind of acknowledgement, including a verbal *thank you*. Achieving the next level, we enter Divine Compassion. This stage allows us to acknowledge the energy of Compassion with the divine Wisdom that there is No-thing wrong and that there is No-thing that we need do to fix anything. We become the compassionate observer, wearing the cloak of Unconditional Divine Love and radiating our love-light waves as a free gift to those who are willing to tap into them without the anchors of expectation of outcome.

We briefly explored the energy of forgiveness earlier and we begin to understand that this energy is but the opening of the gateway to the path. From the Divine Feminine perspective to move into the act of forgiveness requires the strong support of human compassion. Immersed in Duality, we only perceive the wrongness of things and the hurtful actions we suffer at the hands of others. We wrap ourselves within the cloak of victim hood. By clearing the field of the emotional explosives through the human act of forgiveness we take back our power of Self. Wallowing in the pond of victim-hood and suffering, shatters our structure and we lose parts of ourselves within the illusion of separation and un-love. Taking back parts of our true nature that we have allowed to be taken from us enables us to reclaim our wholeness and releases us from the illusion of un-worthiness and depravations. It cleans the connecting links to our Soul partners and allows deeper, intimate communication strengthening the symbiotic relationship.

Once we step back into the wholeness of Self-realization, we gain clarity, presenting us with the inner peace we so desperately seek. From this achieved platform, we can then move into the high road of acceptance, surrender and Unconditional Love. This launching pad jars and propels us into the powerful choice of taking an active step towards 'Walking the Talk'.

DNA number 12—El-Shadai—The Ultimate Divine God Layer

The last God strand announces to the Universe the presence of God within US. Activation of this line opens the private line of full communication with the Divine within. Recognizing and embracing this aspect completes the wiring of the circuit. No obstacles or blockages can remain when this line within the network in our human-soul-being has been plugged in and activated. The final master switch can now be thrown, allowing all transmissions clear communication to every minute particle of our Being.

Only a very small number of Soul-humans have been able to reach this level of open communication where all twelve branches are in full operation. The one who is known to have walked this path of enlightenment is the one called Jesus of Nazareth. It is important to remember that when one line is blocked, it causes static in all the other lines and clear communication between departments cannot be achieved. The illusionary messages that are heard are full of garbled static frequencies and the Ego-Self is the only one who pretends to understand it. It is to be noted that by merely chanting the names of the DNA strands in meditation repeatedly will not activate the lines. Everything is linked like a massive spider web, or branches of a tree and one tiny speck of dust and one single knot will bend and distort the message. It creates dark assumptions within existing heavy belief systems that only feed the Ego even more.

PART FOUR

The Construction Platform

CHAPTER ONE

Transition

Transition within human perception can be accepted as a process of metamorphoses where one state morphs, changes or mutates into another state of being. At this point we have been given a major part of the information regarding to the twists and turns of the multiple levels of transition from a three-dimensional human to an enlightened, ascending prototype. It provides us with the many potential choices of which path to take. The Goddess Path is only one branch of the multiple pathways available for every traveler's choice.

The rewiring and adjustment will continue for many more lifetimes for the majority of the human population. It is a complex undertaking for each Soul-Human symbiotic partnership and it takes a huge amount of energy to maintain the momentum of the transition from one reality to the next. The messages sent to us continually repeat that every strand within creation as we know it has to undergo the alchemy of metamorphoses and transmutation and that NO—one will be left behind. All anchors within the three-dimensional reality of matter and duality will be lifted in accordance with each progression of the Shift. Each individual person on the Earth-Plane monitors and controls his or her own rate of transformation and creates a personal departure time. Some will choose a private and personal flight into transition while others might prefer a group departure. To assist with the multitude and variety of choices, angelic guides have been assigned to monitor and guide the ascension traffic. To help each traveler, these angelic guides assign additional teachers, healers and human guides to those who request aid.

Any and all assistance must be requested, for the angelic group cannot by-pass Free Will.

Unlike the Mini-Miner story, the human transformation does not happen instantaneously within a short time span. Like the analogy of the deep sea diver, or the Lotus stalk, we need to float and rise gradually through the different depths and keep our sight on the light above as a coveted destination. On the way, we are given the opportunity to mindfully release and detach ourselves from all the anchoring mental and emotional chains of duality that stretch all the way back to our entrance into the Earth realm.

The Master switch cannot be thrown until all the wires have been strung according to the new blueprint of the second creation. This work is now in progress and it is time for us to take responsibility and take on the mantle of our own engineering and healing team. It is time to assess and monitor our own journey with full awareness of the rise in Consciousness. Now that we are aware what the journey entails, we can begin our climb up the ladder of evolution with awakening knowledge and wisdom. At each rung, there is a possibility of manifesting a potential where a minor switch can be activated. Imagine completing the wiring and all the appropriate electrical plugs in one room of a new house and finally being able to turn on the lights in that particular room. The light beams from this location may spill out into the hallway and illuminate the areas still under construction, revealing the existence of unseen blockages and bringing more clarity and assistance in the rebuilding process. We need the illuminating beams of light particles to help us 'see' the doors of transition that are available to us at each level of our journey, leading to the next platform of evolution.

One of the first messages for those of us who choose to step on the ladder is that the karmic wheel is slowing down and eventually will come to a full stop for everyone. The records are still being kept and the ledgers updated, but the debit column was eliminated the moment the agreement came into play. Rather than karma being deferred, the effects of karmic behavior occur instantly, becoming an immediate cause and effect action. This means that we cannot bank our debts for the next incarnation any longer, for that option has been terminated with the agreement of the Shift. Each reincarnation for those on the ladder will be co-planned with a supporting team, with the focus on clearing all the karmic debts recorded as still *owing* in the Akash. Every record and ledger has to be cleared before we can enter the final entry gate into the higher dimensional world. Each time we have achieved a cleansing, we are reborn with a different structural configuration that pulses in sync with a resonating environment of existence.

Stepping on the ladder acknowledges our choice to take full responsibility as a spiritually awakened adult. While in human form, we are still subjected to the various temptations of the environment we live in and our job is to make the choices of a mature spiritual Being. We are passengers on the same ship, going towards the same destination and have the choice of traveling in the bowels of Spaceship Earth, or we can enjoy the ride within the comfort of the First-class deck.

When we choose to transition from an unawakened human to a spiritually inquiring mindset we take our first steps of growth like a baby who learns to walk. We begin to perceive the world around us through a different set of glasses. Having released a few layers of emotional baggage, our reactions and responses to any negative actions follow a different route. It moves from a heavy emotion, such as anger, to a response based on higher thought patterns of detachment, tolerance, compassion and acceptance. We walk in mindfulness of our environment and see our fellow humans as our brothers and sisters who have not yet chosen to step on the ladder. We are still cloaked in the human mantle and are presented with the challenges of interacting with others who are not on the same path. This is a great opportunity to exercise human compassion and forgiveness towards our fellow men and earthly family members. Mastering these bridging energies elevate us into the next step of detached compassion, where we eventually embrace Divine Compassion. This action triggers the DNA and stimulates the gears of the Merkabah, turning the switch to transition into the first layers of the Light-Body.

Consciously, we initiate our different choices regarding our daily lives and strive to focus on healing the energies of Self-Love by promoting a healthier life style that affects our mental, emotional, physical and spiritual being. This brings in peace of mind and prepares us for the next transition into another platform of the ladder. Each consequential rung brings us greater opportunities of transmorphation, propelling us into the next phase in this remarkable journey. Remember, the ladder does not exist in a linear time, therefore, the steps, or platforms can be accessed at many different levels during our human lifetimes.

One of the most challenging areas we have to face throughout the journey is the field of Duality. Within this matrix, a part of the Mass Mind is immersed in the illusion of the separation of the sexes. One of the heaviest strands is the unawakened awareness of the genderless state of the Universal Mind. Unless the balance of the male-female energy is achieved within each of us, we cannot access the final doorway to enlightenment. The renowned Nelson Mandela shared his clarity with, "*Freedom cannot be achieved unless women have been emancipated from all forms of oppression . . . Our endeavors must be about the liberation of the woman, the emancipation of the man and the liberty of the child.*"

Duality is a state of being that is so familiar to us that our mental and emotional bodies have difficulty accepting its removal from our reality. We have been introduced to the appearance of the neutralizing component of Triality, and again are presented with a list of choices. Some of us have begun to create a daily mantra to help us deal with this dilemma. We consciously and intentionally choose to break the brain-washing chains and remind ourselves that there is *No-thing wrong, No-thing is broken and No-thing needs our meddling nature of trying to fix things for others.* Opening the door to the non-duality platform shows us the layers of human thought patterns of emotional detachment of neutrality and unlocks the doors to the higher vibrational DNA strands. This third bridging component leads the way into the neutral zone, which is the exit point out of the duality harbor.

It is also important that we keep ourselves continually vigilant and conscious of the Ego-persona. The Ego will try to use every persuasive argument to prevent its demotion from being in control of the pilot seat to the role of a support team member. To initiate the transition of the Ego we have to examine every department it controls. We know that Fear is the controlling power that feeds the Ego conglomerate and it is one of the major challenges of human life. Facing our human fears with courage and determination will slowly erode the Ego's hold upon our daily life. It helps in clearing the chakra engines when we boldly walk the path without the fear of FEAR itself.

The first successful transition will find the Ego out of its position of control and into a supporting role. In this role, the Ego is expected to generate the power necessary to strengthen the awareness of the Self. Using the scenario of the spaceship Enterprise of the Star Trek saga, the Ego is sent down to take on the job of the engineer in charge of providing the energy to power the spaceship. Once we take back our seat as the captain on the bridge, we have gained the maturity to take a firm stand and claim our place within the fabric of Divine Creation. With this choice, we choose to no longer hover behind the persuasive, illusionary actions of the Ego. We ground ourselves firmly and stand as a strong mature lighthouse taking full responsibility of our actions and decisions as the captain of the ship. This shift prepares the Ego to accept that with the demise of Duality, it too must face extinction at some point, for it is an integral grounding strand of Duality. Remember that Duality cannot, and does not exist in the higher dimensional states of consciousness; therefore, it is impossible for the Ego to survive within the higher realities. As we reach the higher platforms, a broad band of frequencies penetrate the auric fields and our maturing light-body begins to exude more and more light from the heart and crown centers. Its pulsing brilliance will eventually over-light the shadowiness of the Ego when our spaceship engages the hyper-drive that propels us out of the Duality realms. Keep in mind that shadows cannot exist in beams of radiating light.

Seven locks were created within the human construct as part of anchoring the system in the field of Duality and each is wired to all layers of the body. Earlier we learned about one of the locks, that which causes separation, abandonment and rejection within the Root Chakra, which is imprinted upon each human at birth. Like a foetus in the womb, we are cradled in a warm, watery world that allows us to safely grow and prepare the body vessel. Upon birth, every baby is subjected to the trauma of being pushed and forcefully expelled, from a comfortable space into an alien world, where the restrictions of Duality are invoked. The baby is immediately bombarded with the energies of separation and abandonment, instantly anchoring it in the field of Duality. It is wrenched from the soothing sound of the mother's heartbeat and the loving embrace of the womb, establishing the tangled knot of human suffering. This grounding lock is part of the inheritance of our past lives carried from template to template, rooting ever deeper into our structure. Every existing knot within every layer of our construct has to be untangled and brushed before any transition can be initiated.

Remember that we choose our parents when we plan our reincarnation back onto the Earth-plane. They are the Souls who have agreed to play the roles of the main supporting characters as our human care-givers upon the stage of our lives. We wrote and scripted our own destiny with layers of potentials and possibilities of paying off our karmic debt load within each life time. We usually script the starting point of the process as early as the womb stage. During the gestation period, the unborn baby hears and feels the emotions and thought patterns of the parents and these strands are imprinted, and stamped upon the developing consciousness of the child. This energetic baggage becomes part of the karmic luggage to be experienced whenever the personality is ready to deal with it.

The messages continue to urge us to dig deeper into the anchoring emotional field, for even the tiniest speck of darkness will prevent the complete harmony required to power the Light Body of ascension. With this in mind, we present you with the analogy of the dandelion root. The dandelion is a very tenacious plant, and considered a noisome weed by many societies. Its multitude of seeds floats on the wind currents and has the ability to root in almost any kind of soil. Once established, it is a challenge to eradicate. The smallest, tiniest piece of root that has not been dug out and removed will re-germinate and grow into a full, sturdy plant in a very short period of time. The deepest and darkest parts of our emotions that are still hidden within our biology are similar to the over-looked little root.

Every human has a set of parents and their presence in our lives is taken for granted. Forgiving our parents is therefore not a natural emotion, it is a hidden, and a deeply ingrained root often undetected in our relationship issues. Uprooting it is a major essential step, for it releases us from this ancient bondage and terminates our relationship with resentment, un-love, blame and guilt patterns. Thanking the Soul of a parent for its loving contribution to help us clear our karmic ledgers is a powerful erasing energy. These radical actions have a domino-like effect, because it provides the energetic push that creates a healing, diluting wave from birth to birth, along both past, present and future lines. Parental behavior and emotional patterns that we have learned, accepted and carried with us throughout our life times are often an unconscious, hidden root part. Like the dandelion root it will re-grow, sending deeper tendrils of blockages into the cellular structure of the physical body, as well as the emotional and mental bodies. When allowed to grow unchecked, this ivy-like growth will eventually cover and hide the key-holes that open the dimensional gates to enlightenment and hide the road to transition from our sight.

Releasing and detaching from the lashings of heavy emotions begin to have a remarkable effect on the personality. The changes are subtle, and when we allow it to flow and follow the currents of the shift, we find ourselves entering an amazing world of self-discovery. We realize that we have begun to evolve and morph into a different person when suddenly we wake up one day and discover that the darker emotions such as anger or revenge do not exist any longer in our mental and emotional body. When we encounter a personality that gives us feelings of discomfort and dislike, we realize we have been shown a mirror image of our selves. This provides an excellent option to reach for the higher understanding that the mirror reflection provides us with insights into our shadow layers. This sense of clarity allows us to heal this particular behavior, eradicating our impulsive need to retaliate with anger, dislike or animosity. Gradually we become conscious of the fact that we have begun to step out of the Duality drama stage and have chosen to be part of the audience instead.

With conscious choice, the old persona faces its demise and transitions into an awakened human who begins the journey with a renewed sense of excitement and determination. Like a new-born babe we begin our halting steps out of the first layers of Duality, transitioning onto the next platform of the evolutionary ladder. Be aware that there is a grieving period where we mourn the departure of our old self. It is a human right to walk the shadow paths of grieving and the sense of loss. This emotional layer will eventually dissipate like the morning mist when the dawn of enlightenment is like the golden rays of the Great Central Sun that burn the fog away.

Chapter Two

The Chrysalis Rebirth

The changes that we are experiencing are very complex in nature and it presents many challenging choices of re-educating our thought patterns. Once again, the Goddess is providing us with a parallel analogy of the intriguing life cycle of the caterpillar, to assist us in our thirst for comprehension.

The caterpillar spends its whole life crawling on the branches of trees and bushes, munching its way through a variety of flowers and leaves. Its world revolves around the experiences it derives from the environment around its crawling capability, and it has no concept of any other way of life. A crawling caterpillar has to deal with many fears and dangers. It often has to shoulder suffering during its existence, as it inches its way over rough bark, jagged pebbles or falling branches. Then one day in its short life span, the caterpillar experiences the urge to find a safe and quiet place where it begins to spin a cocoon around itself. It completely encloses and locks itself in a tight shell. Within the stillness of this space, the caterpillar surrenders its very being, its caterpillar structure. We could almost say that it enters a deep meditative dream state of transition and we know it as the metamorphoses of Chrysalis. In this cocooned stillness, the caterpillar begins to unravel its physical structure, melting down and dissolving into a thick blob of living, pulsing DNA molecules. Its basic living essence is still present but is now undergoing the remarkable, magical alchemy of Chrysalis. This living essence pulses into restructuring and reconfiguring DNA particles creating a brand new matrix. Using the additional harvested chemical compounds of everything it has consumed as a caterpillar, its cellular matrix is transformed into the shape of an exquisite butterfly. When it emerges out of the cocoon, the butterfly or moth becomes aware that it has a different body, one that has wings and can fly where ever it wants. It no longer remembers being a caterpillar and flies into its new life, experiencing the wind currents and the brightness of the sun. It now consumes sweet flower nectar instead of chewing hard and fibrous leaves. A caterpillar who only knows how to crawl cannot exist in the higher realms of air, and the butterfly has no interest in returning to the restrictive life of a crawling caterpillar.

We are the human lotus seedlings, the human Mini Miners and the human caterpillars. At this crossroads of our journey we are aware of the rewiring within our multi-level body layers and begin to wonder where the next level will take us. The Goddess Quan Yin has gifted us with an analogy of a human Chrysalis experience if we choose to walk this Goddess pathway. For the human vessel, it is a much more complicated and intense procedure because the human-Soul structure consists of many layers that exist in different dimensional frequencies. It takes a strong sense of determination and commitment to enter this particular method, for it requires surrendering within a deep meditative state.

The first step is to gain a deeper understanding of what the metamorphosis of chrysalis and the cocoon stages mean for the human caterpillar. The Harmonic Convergence agreement opened the canopy, the window, through which we can see the potential of the human 'butterfly' and discover that we can be much more than a human biped of flesh and bone.

The following is a sequential rendition of possibilities of manifesting the next potentials of metamorphoses, based on the chrysalis adventure. It requires the involvement of all five elements: earth, air, fire, water and the ethers

Our biology depends upon water currents that flow in our blood stream, lubricating and hydrating every cell in the body. Water provides the environment where all the elements interact and work with each other. It is the major communication link that carries not only essential nutrients, but also sound frequencies and is a strong conductor for electrical currents. We exist as electrically charged beings that derive our sustaining power from the generating sources within the chakra system and the Merkabah structures.

Scientific experiments conducted by various scientists have revealed amazing connections between the emotional vibrations and sound frequencies upon molecular structures of matter, particularly water molecules. One experiment conducted by Dr. Masaru Emoto, the famed Japanese author and entrepreneur, provided proof without a doubt that our emotionally charged thought patterns have a significant effect. Dr. Emoto began by examining the molecules of different water sources and noted the different patterns. Under high powered microscopes, he noted that samples from a polluted water source had water crystals of irregular shapes, as compared to the ones taken from a clear water source which exhibited a snowflake-like configuration. He also studied the effect of thought patterns upon water. He requested a group of people to collectively send heavy, hateful, angry and unhappy thoughts to a jar of water and then asked the group to send happy, joyful and loving thoughts to another jar. He photographed and captured the amazing results. The crystal molecules of the sad jar had deformed shapes similar to those formed by the dirty water, while the ones from the loved jar showed distinctively beautiful crystalline formations.

Another scientist observed this phenomenon from a different angle with the same remarkable results. To show the visual effects, he injected a minute amount of white sand particles in water, changing it into a cloudy liquid, then began to expose it to various sound frequencies. The sand particles immediately responded to the stimulation, forming precise geometric clusters in the solution, leaving spaces of clear water in between. These shapes are known as the platonic solids and form basic harmonic patterns when a fluid is subjected to various sound frequencies. As the scientist raised or lowered the frequency of the sound, the sand shape reconfigured and seems to adapt itself to the vibration of each sound. He noted that it shape-shifted into the most intricate, exquisite, crystalline mandala pattern in response to the higher harmonious musical frequencies. On the other hand, heavy-metal musical notes showed an uneven, often distorted blob-like pattern. Note how our body feels when listening to music we love, compared to sounds we hear as intrusive, uncomfortable and at times, even fearful.

The quantum energies involved in the creation of matter are now thought of as having fluid-like properties that are the energetic manifestation of the Universal Mind. This vibration shifts the fluid into geometric patterns, similar to that of snowflakes. This geometric phenomenon was discovered in the nucleus of the atom by a researcher known as Dr. Moon. His experiments concluded that everything we see and experience is an energy vibration. We may assume then that thought patterns are energy vibrations and the frequency will affect the sacred geometric shapes within the fluidity of our cellular configurations.

This irrefutable proof of our connections to the universe around us is giving us a multitude of choices. Our biology is a kind of cellular library that catalogues and stores perfect copies of every thought, every word, emotion and action we go through in our present life. Knowing that our very emotional thought patterns affect our molecular structure and that it has the potential of steering us towards health or illness, may direct us to a different way of life. Accumulated blockages, referred to as toxic mentality interrupt the flow of subtle, nourishing energies within the body, causing disharmony that eventually manifests into dis-ease, an unhealthy situation for all body parts. Accepting and changing our thought patterns by embracing the words of light discussed earlier, is the start button that engages the engines of transition. Exposing our body to higher thought patterns by stepping into the action of Self-love and harmony, we allow our biology to reconfigure into healthier cellular structures that resonate to the higher vibrations of existence. It is a major step towards detaching from Duality Consciousness and it affects the rewiring of the entire system. The more crystalline the molecular structure, the clearer the pathways of communication and it reduces the static within the wiring system.

Having adjusted our thought patterns we are now ready to enter the alchemy of the chrysalis cocoon stages. The Goddess has compiled a series of scenarios to help us experience the emotions of complete surrender of the physical structure of biology within three cocoons. Deep meditation is the first doorway we enter, in order to wrap ourselves within the stillness of an alternate state. An alternate meditative state is the space between the thought waves where silence exists. Within the silence lies the connecting link to the High Mind and the High Heart. The High Mind and the High Heart are junction points that connect to the Source field of Unity Consciousness. This link is the line that transcends the dimensional veils and takes our consciousness to a higher vibrational frequency. The cocoon stages cannot be reached unless we truly accept and acknowledge the existence of this space and the Unity Source Field link within us.

When the caterpillar is inside its cocoon, it is completely isolated and detached from all outside interference of its former life. We as humans need to enter this stage as well. Our human cocoon is a circle of silence and acts like an invisible shell around us when we detach ourselves from the quagmire of human emotional dramas. It does not mean that we isolate ourselves from daily life interactions with others around us. We have only chosen to enter a different category in which we become the quiet listener and the compassionate observer, instead of a vocal and active player in the human drama. We have found the stillness in between the chain of thoughts that is the entrance into the Matrix of non-duality.

Surrendering our consciousness into a deep meditative state, we can enter the first cocoon. It is coined the Golden cocoon, and it deals with releasing the attachments to our physical biological matter. Within the stillness of the cocoon, we are encouraged to surrender and experience the sensation of a melt down to an unstructured mass just like the caterpillar in its cocoon state. Here we allow the complete untangling and unravelling of the 3-D Ego-control-self. As the caterpillar surrenders its form, so too, do we liquefy and dissolve our dark emotional and mental bodies. These heavy particles are like the leaves and buds that the caterpillar has consumed and its chemical compounds are utilized in creating a new frame. In the same manner, we extract and harvest the wisdom from each painful experience as the new flavorings to be added in our next evolutionary structure. The human life is a very complicated cycle and involves daily bombardment of emotions and thought patterns that can reach stormy waves, which in turn may disrupt or even break the shell of the sensitive human cocoon. The major challenge for the human is to maintain the silence and emotional isolation of the cocoon phenomena within the stormy drama of daily life.

Surrendering to the energies of potentiality means the dissolving of all Duality-based thought patterns that are the foundations of human behavior patterns. The act of surrender, detachment and expectations of outcome changes our perception of the Self and our relationship with everyone and everything around us. We begin to perceive the world in which we live in a different light and as a result, we are allowing our old selves to disintegrate and 'die' just like the caterpillar that surrenders to the death of its old shape. There is an initial sense of grieving when we step into this state. It is a human right to embrace the emotion of grief for the loss of the old self or loved ones. It is a valued experience for the Soul partner for the Soul has no concept of the emotional state of the sadness of grieving.

When we submerge ourselves in this deep awareness, we begin to discover the vital roles that the four elements are playing within our biology. The disintegration procedure involves the merging and acceptance of the Oneness with the elements and the reconfiguration of the chakras. The chakra junction points, between biology and spirit-Soul-Self are redirected and repositioned in response to the changes we have initiated when entering the state of Chrysalis.

The caterpillar body undergoes changes to its molecular structure from density to a lighter liquid form. Upon achieving this stage, it submits itself to the re-creation and re-configuration into a lighter body framework that has the ability to fly into the sky. In the case of the human biology, every particle must be purified and transformed into a higher, lighter frequency. It too, can be reconfigured and refracted back into a lightbody that can fly and soar in the Ultimate Universe. To achieve this state, we have to submit to the practice of alchemy that transforms our carbon—based biology into a silicon crystalline configuration. Silicon crystals have a greater capacity to hold light and therefore, become the matrix of the lightbody. Silicon crystals are capable of carrying greater and higher magnetic energies. Our carbon based biology is powered with electrical energies and needs to be elevated into silicon components that will raise our structure into a higher frequency of a magnetic system.

The vibrations of our emotions, attitudes and thought patterns that govern our actions are the very channels that affect our evolutionary progression. The speed, progress and direction of the metamorphoses of Chrysalis are in direct correlation to the choices we make, based on the gift of Free Will.

Once we initiate the melt-down process, we allow the elements to merge within the safety of the human cocoon chamber, thus entering the fluid state of Oneness. In this alternate state, we sense the liquification of the physical body and perceive it as a golden plasma-like liquid that is overseen by the male energy. The work of releasing and cleansing of cellular memory begins with the tools provided by the elements. All the elements work together as a team and coordinate each action taken. When we fully accept that we are one with the elements and acknowledge our oneness with the planet, we ignite the activation of DNA strand number four that connects the communication link to the Divine Planetary Essence. The surrender to Oneness should not be mistaken with loss of identity. On the contrary, all the qualities of Oneness are added as a loving support to the personality, enhancing its individual unique quality.

The water molecules provide the vehicle currents for the electrical charges within all the elements to wash and cleanse the stored heavy blockages in every cell. The heart-water-crystal-core is the pulsing engine that propels the elemental currents throughout the body channels and assists the cleansing sequence. Air, as the living breath, powers the sound frequencies generated by the throat to reveal the location of deeper core issues. Harmonious sound frequencies reconfigure the geometric shapes within the cellular liquid, raising its energetic intensity. The higher frequencies of the geometric shapes have the capability and capacity to release and disassemble the tangled core issues. Meanwhile, the Fire element maintains the healthy temperature the body needs. At the same time, its assignment is to utilize the pulsing Kundalini fire rising in the prana tube to increase the cleansing and purifying of this energy conduit.

The cleansed, golden living essence will flow into the second cocoon. It is a silvery, platinum cocoon chamber saturated with the female, loving, nurturing and compassionate essence. As the golden liquid enters, it merges with the silvery energetic flow, and it is stirred into a new mixture of non-gendered oneness, changing into a silvery-gold weave. It is another step towards disengaging from the Duality mentality. This cocoon deals with the restructuring of the chakra system, inserting the Divine Love component that spirals all six chakra colors into the seventh strand of the heart center.

All four elements are put to work again in this cocoon. Each Chakra likewise, is cleansed continually by the coordinated effort of the four elements. The combined, colorful ribbons are collected into a rainbow-colored spiraling link that is drawn into the Heart core. The rainbow spectrum is in turn refracted by the love-water-crystals in the heart chamber into a unified beam of white light. This higher frequency can be accelerated by infusing it with waves of harmonious heart song and the bridging emotions of forgiveness, love and compassion.

Having achieved this frequency of being, we now have gained access into the crystal doorway of the crystal cocoon. This cocoon is very different than the previous two cocoons. The entrance is a crystal ante-chamber, similar to the top of a lighthouse where its walls are made up of seven rotating, crystal, window-like panels. The combined liquid-light essence from the previous two cocoons is tasked with the cleansing of all seven panels, as a prerequisite to entering the core chamber of the crystal cocoon.

The panels are coated with the remaining distortions that dim the glow of the light quotient acquired so far. Shifting, shadowy reams of heavy thought patterns, painful, dark emotions and stacked rows of unmindful, duality words of Ego, cover each panel. The panels are to be faced one at a time, to be cleared of the dark smudges, with all the tools gained up to this point. The strongest cleansing agents that are available for our use are the frequencies of sound, assisted by the appropriate features of the elements, such as washing windows with water and soap. The blowing strength of the wind can scatter the dark clouds; the scouring of the earth minerals; and the scorching, transmuting force of fire, contribute to the purging of the panels. Once again, the four elements come to the rescue with their supporting loving embrace.

As each panel is cleared, it transmits vibrating light particles that illuminate the chamber with increasing crystalline light. The moment all seven panels are cleared, they radiate a pulsing, spiraling beam of light in all directions, transforming the ante-chamber into one crystal gate.

In order to grasp the final stages of the alchemy of Chrysalis, it is necessary to detach from linear thinking and step into an alternate dimensional reality. It is not an easy endeavor, because it is not compatible with the human five sensory perceptions when we immerse into the evolutionary state of non-duality. Once we are comfortable with the alternate thought pattern, we have the potential of greater awareness and acceptance of the transformative attributes of the crystal cocoon chamber. This allows the entrance of the sixth and higher senses into our awakened Consciousness, enabling our inner sight to gain clarity.

The crystal gate admits us into a vast multifaceted crystal dome. In the center is an egg-shaped crystal cocoon that houses our new fetal body, suspended in a liquid, crystalline embryonic fluid that contains the fifth element, the vibration of the ethers. Held safely in this crystal womb, the metamorphic alchemy begins the reconfiguration of our carbon-based cellular structure into a crystalline silicone one. The rate of the transmutation correlates with the level of consciousness achieved. The Over-Soul team monitors the growth, magnetization and expansion of the light particles and will initiate the necessary adjustments in the chamber when required.

Maintaining a continual strong and deep breath of life is mandatory to fuel and energize the passage from cocoon to cocoon. A big percentage of dimensional space is filled with the element of air through which weaves the dimensional fifth element, the ethers. As we purposefully increase the volume of the breath, we begin to access the adamantine particles of Creator Light that reside within the ethers. When we begin to spiral the breath in the shape of the infinity symbol from the heart, we accelerate the currents of Divine Creator energy. The spiral breath focuses, sending the breath into the soul-star on the in-breath and loops the earth-star on the out-breath crossing over the heart. This establishes a powerful figure eight pattern. This pattern encourages the integration of escalating numbers of life-code seed atoms provided by the Over-Soul. When we consciously engage the spiral breath, we gain the ability to reach the still point of the atom-seed, causing it to increase the magnetization and integration of Creator Light particles. Magnetization of all particles is important to increase the electrical power pulses required to maintain and sustain the engine of evolution. The infinity breath allows the Light particles to accumulate in the Heart center, and in turn widens the channels into the Pineal master gland. In the Pineal, the light particles are filtered into the brainwave synaptic field according to the level of achieved vibration. When we choose to allow the ongoing transfiguration of the new structure and wiring systems, the changes within us become more and more evident in the crystal cocoon chamber.

The rate of recalibration of the Merkabah, the light-vehicle that is manifesting around the cocoon, is also directly correlated with the progress of the atomic readjustment of the matrix of the crystalline fetus. The first geometric figure of the Merkabah is the hexahedron, which is a cube shape. Raising the vibrational frequencies of this grounding layer energizes the Tree-of-Life and roots it into the heart of the developing avatar body. This completes the circuit formed by the lines of communication among the grounding DNA groupings of one to nine, two to eight and three to six.

The second geometric shape encapsulates the first, and it is the icosahedron that begins to flush out any remaining obstructive particles still floating in the system. Once cleared, the next geometric container, the star tetrahedron, continues to raise the frequency by bringing in the neutralizing fire that transforms the Ego-Will into Divine Will and further encourages the move out of Duality. At the same time, the energy of the star tetrahedron, upon reaching the appropriate level becomes androgynous, merging male and female energies into Oneness that was initiated within the platinum cocoon.

When all the geometric shapes have clicked in place and are pulsing with increasing speed, the whole structure takes on the configuration of the blazing Chariot of Fire. It is the recalibrated and magnetized space-suit of the lightbody that resonates in higher vibrational frequencies and has the capability of navigating the interdimensional highways.

Choosing to enter the Chrysalis phenomenon changes the symbiotic relationship between the Soul and the human partner. The newly increased vibrational frequencies begin to flow through the changed chakra junction points and reach a higher manifestation of the symbiotic combined structure. The potentiality of the complete interface of cellular biology to the true light body matrix of the Soul has become a reality in the inner crystal cocoon chamber. This developmental shift is a complicated endeavor and it is not expected for anyone to be able to reach this destination in one life time. The potential of possibility is there, however the intense energies involved and the cost to the human body are very high and not to be taken lightly. It may take many turns of reincarnation for humanity to enter the final stretch.

In its finishing stages, the internal make-up of the new Soul-Human being consists of balanced, lighter strands of light that begin to emit a more harmonious song, and the human caterpillar is ready to enter the final stages of Chrysalis. The crystal lotus seed has germinated within the crystal waters of the new Heart core and is about to bloom into a brilliant, sparkling crystal lotus. In full bloom, the crystal lotus represents the new flower of life for its expanded crystal petals reflect the full spectrum of creator light. The new model of the interdimensional human-avatar is about to emerge from its cocoon. The finish line is in sight, but the long awaited time for the unveiling of this new model is yet to be determined, for there is time allotted for last minute changes. Each emerging occasion is a personal happening based on the rate of transmutation and the choice of Free Will.

CHAPTER THREE

Spaceship Earth

At this time in history, it is a given that the Earth is going through its own evolution. As a spaceship for humanity and all the living Earth's essences, it is a huge undertaking and can be a frightening experience for those who are unawakened. As our vibrational bodies grow and change, so does the Earth body, for its structure closely resembles the human vehicle construct. The Earth is a watery, blue planet and the four elements flow and blow within it the same way that the bloodstream and air circulate within us. The globe is encapsulated within layers of protective energetic structures similar to the Merkabah around the human form. A chakra system is also present within the Earth's mantle, and these energy vortexes are undergoing the necessary restructuring and recalibration. In compliance with the requirements of the Shift, as the power centers of the seven chakras have been redirected and merged into the heart center of the human framework, the same changes apply to the Earth's chakra system. The four elements within the Earth respond similarly to the ebb and flow of the emotional waves of the resident Mass Consciousness.

Gaia, the Earth Mother has put herself in her 'cocoon', and we are in it since we are part of her cellular structure. The process of Chrysalis has begun for the Earth body, and we as the living particles upon her surface, are participants in her evolutionary climb. Gaia's chakra system is complying with the Great Shift mandate and has begun its journey of recalibration. It is for us to note that, as she changes so do we. As we grow into enlightenment, so does she.

It was revealed before that the changing role of the heart center is the most important factor that is relevant to the reconstruction process. The Heart Chakra is considered to be the Divine Love Portal, and the core of the love-body. The Earth's Love-Portal is the largest heart energy center in the physical realms, and it is largely powered and balanced by the water element. It encompasses a large area in the Pacific Ocean, with the Hawaiian Islands being the Northern boundary, and the French Polynesian Islands marking the southern boundary of the Earth's heart Center.

For the Great Shift to reach the high acceleration required, it is not only necessary to anchor the highest quotient of Divine Love energies within this vortex, but also to clear it of all debris and pollutants. At this point, we are aware that the chakras contain different numbers of rotating cones that are funnels of energy. The Earth's Heart Chakra follows the same structure of twelve main cones. These cones are slightly different in that they open outwards to form a central ring. The ring is made out of Love Water crystals and there are twelve crystals in each cone. At the base of the cones lies the Love Crystal of the Heart. It is a large water crystal that anchors the Love-body, serving as an interface between the Love-Body and the Light-Body. Crystal water pathways link each cone to the inter-dimensional portals at galactic and cosmic levels.

Many of the original wounds from the initial time of Separation and sense of Abandonment are carried within the cellular heart memories. These discordant Soul memories are part of the debris that must be cleansed and released first through the lower base bodies. Attempting to cut corners and by-pass this process by trying to force the cleansing from the higher dimensional body will only result in creating more blockages in the heart cones. This is the main pathway for the embodiment of the Divine Creator presence in Physical reality or, in other words, the way to bring heaven to Earth.

Our heart energies are the minute rivulets that converge and flow into the Earth's heart center. As we make the effort to cleanse our love pathways, it contributes more and more love water crystals to be added to the Earth's heart love reservoir. It is therefore important for us to increase our efforts in clearing our water ways within the heart as we continue to walk the path of enlightenment within the Earth's realms.

According to the Mayan prophecies, the Earth is entering its next evolutionary path after a twenty-six thousand year span. It is still believed that it is a regular occurring phenomenon. At the culmination of each 26,000 year cycle, the Earth experiences a quantum shift in consciousness. The Mayans saw that this cycle ended on December 21st, 2012.

The big difference this time around is that the Mayan shift coincides with the agreement of the Great Shift in Consciousness. This change has never happened before, and we are the participants of something that is beyond anything that the Creative Energies have experienced. At the beginning of the shift, these changes were very subtle, but it will slowly seep into the High Mind of the Mass Consciousness when different, unpredictable, upheavals begin happening upon the Earth's crust. Coincidentally, the Earth's magnetic field which has been slowly weakening for centuries has suddenly begun to weaken at an increasing rate. When the field is reduced to a zero null-point, it will cause the Earth's magnetic poles to shift. When this happens it may cause additional chaos to occur. The end of 2012 was also the scheduled time for the Earth to shift to a higher dimensional level as part of the agreement of the Harmonic Convergence. Inasmuch as human consciousness was also making a quantum leap, we were permitted to concomitantly accompany Gaia in her move and her decision to ascend.

When Atlantis sank beneath the ocean surface, it took all its heavy vibrational frequencies with it. Water molecules are the carrier vehicles of all the elements, and thus also carry all the heavy vibrational frequencies that were created during the Atlantean era. This heavy water sank together with the land masses of the Atlantian continent and remained deep in the ocean depths to be cleansed and purified over thousands of Earth years. For the last few centuries, the Atlantean water layers have reached the lighter, higher frequencies and have begun their slow rise to the surface of the oceans. The return of Atlantis was promised as a long awaited sign that the change is upon us. Pieces of the ancient land mass will also rise and emerge to the surface, as new land and new islands. Ancient artifacts that have been hidden in the deep chasms have begun to slowly resurface and have begun to stimulate dormant memories in the minds of men.

We have been exploring the effects of massive, worldwide pollution during our times of industrialism and materialism, and it has weighed down the energies of our water particles. It is predictable that this heavy layer must begin to sink, according to the law of energetic gravity. This rotation of energies has created a current and it is gaining strength, creating the necessary under-tow power for change. The waters will cause massive, cleansing hurricanes and tornadoes across the globe as part of the anticipated Earth changes. Keep in mind that the intensity of these occurrences, caused by the four elements is directly correlated to our rise in consciousness and the reactional choices we make as a world population. Our choices as individuals are the wispy threads that are braided into the thick ropes that can change the extent of the turmoil. Once braided, the strands are woven into the tapestry of potentials of the new world.

The churning changes below the surface feeds the spin to raise the frequencies of matter necessary for the voyage through the interdimensional journey. The Earth's magma core is the fireplace that fuels the engine for the changes, while the volcanoes take on the roles of venting pipes to release accumulated pressures. This active restructuring becomes more and more evident along the western coastal regions of the globe, known as the *Ring of Fire*. The increase in volcanic eruptions along this area causes the intense tremors that will shift the tectonic plates below the Earth's surface. When this happens, we know that Gaia has notified us about her intention to shrug out of her old mantle.

As revealed earlier, everything has to be reconstructed and recalibrated into a new space-ship that is capable of navigating the intense energetic ribbons of dimensional space. It is logical therefore, to assume that the Earth's crust must undergo a type of facial surgery. We realize that it cannot be done within one life-time; however, we can influence and temper the force of the elements with our combined choices of increasing the Love energy quotient within the heart. The coming centuries of human history will witness the changing topography of the Earth's surface that will provide very different scenery for our future children and grandchildren.

Time and Space were the Duality, three-dimensional walls that anchored the Earth's reality and have to be dismantled as part of this move. The rise in technology has given us the ability to break through the sound barrier, and we are on the brink of discovering the secrets of surpassing the speed of light. The Etheric Earth has already moved into the next dimensional platform and it is time for the physical Earth to follow suit. The planet is encapsulated in its own version of the Merkabah space-suit that is being recalibrated in preparation for the launch into the dimensional corridors of space.

The Earth's energetic matrix has begun to drift into a plasmic energy layer called the Photon Belt, while at the same time the sun is going through its own magnetic pole shift. The sun and the moon are part of the Earth's three-dimensional harbor and are both responding to the winds of change. The international space-agencies have already encountered many puzzling anomalies in the frequency and strength of solar mass ejections that did not follow the normal patterns observed in the past. Increasing ionic solar storms, and more frequent powerful bursts of Gama rays, have driven the scientists to seek for more answers. These solar activities will continue to create global disruptions in the wireless energy channels we depend upon in our present society until our technology can recalibrate and re-adjust to the changes. The domino effect is in play in all layers, for when one system crashes others will follow suit. As we raise the vibrations within our energetic fields, they trigger wild weather patterns around the globe and noticeably, unusual cosmic acceleration within the known Universe.

The weather patterns are responding to the urgings of the elements and human Mass Consciousness. Cold snowy fronts seem to envelop regions that have not experienced these frigid weather patterns for many decades. Dry, arid regions are flogged by rainstorms, while other areas are turning into deserts. Heat waves with dangerous, rising temperatures cause suffering for the weak and elderly in regions that are not prepared to withstand such conflicting weather patterns.

We have taken a look into the perceived connections of pollution and global warming. Based on spiritual information given to us, we may acquire greater understanding of the rise in temperatures. The Earth's axis has begun its tilt towards a new position, and the melting of the polar ice caps as part of the responsibility of the water element, prepares for the inevitable pole shift. The Earth elements follow suit, with the shifting of the land masses through earthquakes and the rerouting of streams and rivers. The fire element takes on the role of purification and is supported by volcanic eruptions and forest fires. Fire is a powerful hand of alchemy of metamorphosis that transforms and alters everything it touches into ashes. Ash reverts anything into its basic chemical compounds and returns it back home to the basic elemental components of the Earth. The contributing factor of the air element is the wind currents, which act as Gaia's breath of life and forms the powerful force that blows away the dark and heavy cobwebs of emotions we have imposed upon her. Hurricane-force winds are necessary to uproot the pools of stagnated, heavy, shadow energies that have accumulated in different areas around the globe.

The Earth heaves and is determined to shrug itself loose from its tired, old cloak, for Gaia has chosen to enter the path into ascending Consciousness. She has begun to blaze a new track in the etheric corridors of dimensional space. She yearns to go home. What her new coat will look like no one knows, for the end of time as we know it, is shrouded in the mists of infinite, unrealized possibilities.

CHAPTER FOUR

Lotus Petals

The Goddess wishes humanity to know that she will be with us until the end of time and she has pledged her continued support and assistance during our sojourn. She remembers her time on Earth as a human and understands that education and learning are essential parts of growing into responsible adulthood. As part of her educational campaign, she gently showers us with information we need along the road. She calls these road signs, Lotus petals, because of her affinity with the lotus plant, and it is up to each individual to gather these petals or not. For those who have chosen to board the train of transformation, the petals are reminders, or guide posts, with constantly updated information and can even be taken as tools to help us navigate the pathway.

The knowledge presented through each petal helps to erode the powerful grip of Ego-fear energies, for it is said that Fear is but the absence of knowledge and love. Once we have accepted knowledge, we are held accountable and responsible for the acquired information. Having passed the driver education program, we are deemed to be responsible drivers on a busy highway, therefore claiming ignorance when we get into an accident is not acceptable. Through her many human assistants, the Goddess intends to continue to shower our pathway with petals of encouragement, information posts, divine compassion and her intense love for humanity to guide us to grow into responsible and enlightened spiritual adults.

One of the first petals that require our attention is that of Time. Time as we know it, does not exist in the higher dimensions of existence, but we have taken linear time for granted as part of our daily life. In accordance with the Shift, time has accelerated in direct proportion to the increase in vibration. The Earth's population will slowly begin to realize that the 24-hour day passes by much faster than it did previously. For many, it is a gradual manifestation, and it seems as if there is not enough time any longer to complete our chores during a day. As long as we do not get persuaded by the Ego-self to enter the darker energies of frustration and impatience, the acceleration of time is a welcomed road sign along the path. For the enlightened initiate, it becomes a much anticipated time of renewal, excitement, exploration, wonder and magic.

As we slowly move out of, and disengage from the restriction of time and space, we take the next steps out of Duality Consciousness. We wrap ourselves in the cloak of detachment from human drama, of acceptance of neutrality, and we *walk the talk* of Love and Oneness. We are moving along a new track, a different stage, upon which we are choosing to play a new game titled as *the transformative road to enlightenment and ascension.* Roles are being rewritten by our Soul partners and we are learning our updated script moment by moment, as we act out each new line within our NOW reality in our travels. Walking in mindfulness within each NOW moment gives us the opportunity to get acquainted with the energies of higher levels of Consciousness and acclimatize ourselves with the sensations of a different Being.

Reincarnation continues to deposit each Soul-human participant into the appropriate holodeck reality that resonates with his/her achieved vibration. Movement from one level to the next is a possibility within each life time, depending upon the rate of awakening. The pathway or gateway to the higher levels of Consciousness can only be sensed and entered by those who resonate to the frequency of the gate. These gates are neither visible, nor sensed by any who have not reached the corresponding frequencies of Consciousness. The doors to the higher levels are the doors leading out of Duality and anyone who is still mired in Duality can neither see nor pass through the doorways.

Our present levels of Consciousness allow us to only perceive the environment of our existing life, and we cannot move into another floor or holodeck until we resonate with its frequency. For example, when the invading Spanish armada appeared on the horizon of the South American continent, it was not detected by the indigenous population. The vision of large warships sailing on the ocean surface was totally alien to the minds of the native people, and thus their minds could not accept the possibility of such an impossible manifestation. However, a shaman whose sensory perception exceeded those of the masses was able to see the ships. Once he persuaded others that the ships were truly there, the change in frequency of the Mass Consciousness of the native population allowed the tribal warriors to see the approaching, invading naval force.

It is important that we remember the fact that there are many multiple dimensional realms, and all occupy the same space, but at different frequencies. Many of us cannot 'see' or 'sense' the elementals or disincarnated spirits that live amongst us, because like the ships they occupy a different frequency. This strange and unusual anomaly does not apply to some of us who are stepping onto the high roads of Consciousness. Categorizing the unknown as being 'alien' soon loses its impact when we accept the reality of the presence of another state of being. The interdimensional veils grow thinner for those who begin to resonate to the higher realms, and we may begin to become aware and even see, the alternate realities that exist around us.

Moving in sync with the changing waves, the corresponding shift in the spiritual body may trigger a radical turn in behavior patterns and cause a sudden change in the person's life. When a seeker's outlook on life begins to branch out into deeper spiritual awareness of Divine Oneness, it can result in the breakdown of long standing relationships. It is the same energy that results in the distancing of family members. When one partner chooses to walk the path of awakening and the other member does not, it creates an energetic chasm that eventually cannot be bridged. It is then up to the enlightened partner to embrace detached compassion with the full acceptance that the separation and the severance of the relationship is no-ones' fault. The feelings and emotions of anger, blame and guilt do not have a space to anchor to when the heart is full of the light filaments of Unconditional Divine Love.

The institution of marriage that has been accepted through the centuries was the fruit of the human creative mind and thus anchored within the 3D platform. In accordance with the Great Shift, many of the established human ceremonies that are mired in ancient customs and belief systems require a readjustment, re-evaluation of their values and relevance within the changing time of consciousness. The dismantling of these formal institutions is now obvious with the increase in divorce rates and the acceptance of common law living arrangements.

Then one day we wake up with the realization that we, ourselves are on a different road and in a different neighborhood. All of a sudden, it seems as if we have lost touch with our old friends and even family members and to our amazement we accept the situation with the emotion of detached compassion. We live in the same community but begin to feel as if we walk along a different sidewalk. Although we can still communicate and see our neighbours, we feel a sense of remoteness and the strange feelings of alienation from the 3D world around us. We have transcended into another etheric holodeck reality and find that we are more comfortable resonating and connecting with like-minded occupants of the deck. Although we love our Earth family, we discover the growing connectedness and closeness to other people we begin to look upon as our spiritual family. We gravitate towards resonating friendships and partnerships. The potential exists that unawakened family members may choose the path of anger and jealousy and ostracize the spiritual seeker. The challenge for the seeker is to continue to walk the path with the balancing cloak of Unconditional Love with the wisdom that everyone is a child of Light who is on a special Soul-adventure.

Physical changes are a given for those on the journey and this may cause the resurfacing of fear based emotions. Remember that the recalibration process is happening within every cell and every organ of biology. All layers of the body require healing, for a weak vessel will not have the strength required for this challenging journey into unchartered levels of Consciousness. The matter of our biology will experience physical discomfort such as pain in different parts of the body as the cellular structure begins its metamorphoses. It is one of the main issues because it is often visually observed and physically felt. Human health issues are a constant challenge and become more confusing with the influx of contradictory messages, for those on the Spiritual pathway.

Foods we have consumed during our lifetimes are suddenly considered not supportive to the acquired rise in vibration. It comes back to the gift of Free Will. It is an acceptable choice whether we relinquish or delete meat products from our diet. It does not necessarily affect the energetic current of the nourishment our biology requires when we honor our needs for survival. Showing and voicing our gratitude, appreciation and thanksgiving to the various kingdoms for providing us with sustenance raises the vibrational frequencies of anything we choose to eat. On the other hand, when we plunge ourselves into following diets based on the belief that it will elevate us into a higher vibration it affects the energetic structure of the food we ingest. This thought pattern is wrapped in the concept of right or wrong and we play directly into the hands of Duality.

Physical changes of the human body, thus are inevitably noticeable in correlation with the changes within the other body layers. The following is a short sample list of potential manifestations of physical changes within the body. The experiences will take on different forms and manifest with different intensity for each traveler on the path.

- Soreness and sudden stabs of pain in the feet, joints, arms and legs
- Digestive challenges with normally acceptable food products. Inability to consume favorite items and suddenly acquiring taste for different foods.
- Frequent flu-like symptoms are the norm during this journey.
- Allergic reactions that were not experienced before or intensifying of previous symptoms
- Chest pain that might feel like a heart attack
- Painful tightness on the skull, especially at the back of the head in the Medulla Oblongata area.
- Sudden dizzy spells
- Sinus problems
- Different sleeping patterns
- Changes in the five senses, such as hearing unusual frequencies of sound or ability to perceive auric colors, etc.

The list grows longer as we experience the changes within our biology, based upon our commitment to the voyage of the Soul's awakening. It is each person's choice whether to ask for help or to try to face the shift alone. It has been noted, however, that group energy is an incredible powerful source of support that is available to promote healing. Increasing numbers of different energy healers, counselors and therapist are choosing to offer their knowledgeable services, based on their own levels of awareness to any seeker of alternative healing.

The emotional and mental bodies also have to deal with disruptions within thought patterns and unexplainable, unprovoked emotional eruptions along this journey of self-awareness. To many of the traveler, the physical and emotional symptoms can be baffling and puzzling, causing worry, anxiety and possibly fear. These ascension symptoms can take on the illusion of a heart attack or another painful illness and may cause discomfort and anxiety. To some these symptoms have never been experienced, and to alleviate and smooth recurrence of worry and fear, it is advisable to seek medical advice when necessary. To ignore these emotions will only result in an immediate halt and a standstill of the journey. The energies of worry and anxiety are the brakes that put the human vehicle into a stationary position on the Ascension Pathway.

To further assist with health concerns of all the body layers a special group of tools have been collected. To ease the use of these tools, it is hereby presented with an acronym—as a D.R.E.A.M. petal.

D stands for **DETOXIVICATION**, a process of relieving the cells of toxic, unhealthy substances. No matter where it materializes in the body, it causes an unhealthy energy flow. For the physical, there are many herbs provided by Earth's pharmacy to counteract and heal the toxic imbalance. For the mental-emotional body, the art of detoxing involves the mindfulness in our choice of words and our reactions to every encounter in our lives. Blaming anyone, including the self and submerging in guilt are toxic strands that invade the flow of clear energies. For the Spiritual body, toxicity of spiritual competition and Ego are the bars that imprison us in Duality.

R stands for **REST**. The physical body cannot function without adequate rest. Denied of a good night's sleep the internal mechanism of the body works overtime and becomes stressed causing disruptions in the energy flow. Mental rest is required to reduce the bombardment of mental chatter and prevent mental fatigue. Rest for the emotional body is definitely a high priority. Without adequate rest the stability of the emotional energy flow is in jeopardy and leads to mental strain that will affect the whole body. The spiritual body is also in need of a periodic rest period. The mind can be overloaded with the torrent of spiritual messages, teachings and the unrealistic expectations of spiritual advancements. It may trigger a situation where the emotional-mind body is unable to process the overload and collapses into a spiritual emergency.

E stands for **ELIMINATION**. This process goes hand in hand with the detoxing sequence. When we start the detoxing program, we initiate the elimination of the toxins in various parts of the body. We need to remind ourselves that the skin is our biggest organ and many toxins can be eliminated through our pores. Mentally, it will benefit the system to eliminate negative vocabulary and thought patterns from our daily interactions with others and the Self. Consciously eliminating heavy, dark emotions such as anger, the need for retaliation and revenge, resentments and many other congested emotional strands, clears the field for the emotions of Light and Love. Eliminating the coveted, spiritual pedestal of the Guru strips the illusion of spiritual glamour from spiritual expectations.

A stands for **ACTION**. Purposeful action is required to keep the cleansing momentum going. The physical body is built for movement and lack of it creates congestion in the joints and the muscles. The exercises for the mental body can be an enjoyable experience when we chose reading material that is interesting to the mind. The Sleeping Prophet known as Edgar Cayce once said that the mind is the builder. Stimulated, the mind builds the foundation for the creative ideas that in turn, energize the emotional body and assist with focussing more positively on the Self. Spiritual actions, such as participating in spiritual discussions, visiting areas with high vibrations, and attending resonating venues, will keep the spiritual channels in a healthy state.

M stands for **MEDITATION**. The importance of meditation was discussed earlier and it is strongly recommended once again. A meditative state puts the physical body in a state of relaxation that gives all the internal organs an additional rest period. It stills the mind as it lessens the chatter and static of daily intrusions. Within the stillness, the synaptic brain particles are given the opportunity to restructure and strengthen its communication network. Maintaining the stillness for a sustained period of time opens the doors for the emotional body to release its tight hold on past and present traumas, allowing cleansing tears to clear the board. At the same time the spiritual body begins to generate a higher vibration that may propel one into an expansion of Consciousness bringing awareness, wisdom and knowledge.

We are encouraged to walk in this D.R.E.A.M. state as often as we can. It is one of the many tools available to help us in our journey. Any assistance that we encounter is valuable.

We may recall that thought patterns are vibrations and that the spoken or non-spoken word is a powerful tool that can be utilized to release congestion. The bridging word of 'forgiveness' is one of these important tools. The first brick to build this bridge is to acknowledge and face the existence of the causal incident. The challenge we face here is the illusion of the act of 'forgiving'. We voice that we have forgiven, however, we refuse to forget the incident and the actors involved in the drama. The power of the word *'forgiveness'* in this instant is nullified for we restrict its flow by still embracing criticism, blame and by hanging on to the dark illusion of being attacked. It is the over-seen dandelion root that will re-grow into another blockage. Allowed to remain, it festers like an infected wound and eventually affects the physical and mental health of the body. Anxiety attack syndrome, depression and digestive disorders are but a few of the potential symptoms. However, once we completely forgive others and ourselves without any restrictions, we move the mental-emotional body out of victimization and suffering. The fruit of forgiveness is the realization that we have the opportunity to harvest wisdom from the situation. It reveals the power of our true self, the acknowledgement of the, I AM, and shows that the experience is a positive mark on our Akashic records, which moves us out of the necessity of forgiveness. A Spiritual Master summed it up with; *"If you have not forgotten and you are still embracing judgement, you have not forgiven."* In other words, if you keep retelling the story, you continue to feed the drama and the reel keeps rolling over and over again on the screen of your life, perpetuating the imbalance and disharmony.

On another level, a number of Lightworkers have begun to notice the surfacing of hidden gifts within their etheric bodies. These are the psychic strands that we all have, such as clairvoyance or clairaudience that we have not tapped into. Up to this point, we have not utilized the full capacity of our brains. To awaken the dormant brain, the cellular brain synapses are being restrung and rewired to allow activation of more communication channels. Additional brain synapses are required to support the growing communication channels and electro-magnetic fields generated by the increasing utilized capacity of the brain. The Pineal gland, deep inside the brain mass is a master psychic gland and the center of the Crown Chakra. It serves as a gateway for all rays of creation radiated through the etheric element by the angelic realms. The awakening of psychic brain activities correlates to the opening of the dormant parts of the brain. The Pineal monitors and filters the attributes, qualities and virtues of the rays. This prevents overwhelming the synaptic brain circuitry and causing a dangerous power-outage when the system is not yet compatible with the frequencies of the rays.

Our old and ancient customs, habits and belief systems are slowly losing its grip on society as it feels the tug of the departing current of Duality. The following is but a minute drop of potential scenarios that are already stepping into the changing tides.

Monetary systems world-wide already are undergoing massive reorganization of banking methods and trade applications. The world financial empires are beginning to feel the enormity of the potential crash and shift of the illusion of wealth. The use of coinage or paper money is already diminishing and is facing complete eradication within the next few centuries. Having looked at these components, we are still faced with strong Duality energies in present society. There is still an enormous gap between the wealthy and the poor, along with the have and the have-nots, the healthy and the disabled in every walk of human life. However, as humanity begins to respond to the starter button of the Shift, hope is around the corner. Heavy energies such as greed and selfish hoarding of wealth will soon no longer be tolerated by the Higher-Mass-Mind.

Discrimination is an underlying current that runs along deep hidden channels in the minds of men in many countries. In many societies, women are still considered less than human, without any rights and are subjected to humiliating and often violent acts. These strands are only a fraction of the Duality weave, and it is a challenge for the rising Mass Consciousness in its attempts to support the energy of neutrality. The ultimate choice of the individual spiritual walker has the important potential role to tip the scales in favor of balanced neutrality.

The world-wide education system is another arena that requires attention. The subsequent new-born human infants, who are entering the new game-board, are bringing different sets of tools and it may seem as if waves of amazing prodigies have joined the world population. The new human generation will not tolerate the old systems any longer and will strongly demand change. As of the year 2000, every infant born was gifted with the indigo qualities. This means that their main auric color is of the indigo frequency that allows them to instantly tap into many psychic gifts. Many also have demonstrated the abilities of total recall of their past lives and these children have the tendency to confuse and frighten parents who have not yet chosen to awaken. These new children have come in to become our teachers and step into the roles of system busters, for they will insist on the reorganization and restructuring of many old stagnated systems. Their IQ quotient is very high on the scale and at times, will even surpass the latest percentile. Their comprehension of technology often seems miraculous, and it is understandable that these children often do not have the patience for the older and slower energies around them.

The educational methods used to date can no longer serve the need of the new generation. It may come to a critical point where immediate decisions need to be made to prevent the loss of young, highly innovative minds, through neglect and the inability of the old system to rise to the challenge of change. As the Earth rotates into a new vibrational cycle, its inhabitants must strive to resonate with the attained levels of the higher frequencies. The energies of survival begin to present a whole different meaning for the new generation.

As part of the knowledge of quantum physics, it is known that the creation of the Universe is based on mathematics. This is clearly evident with the Fibonacci golden ratio spiral that is found in many structures of living matter, as in the pattern in a shell and the precise structure of the Merkabah. The world has agreed to use a base-ten numerical system in its daily interactions for a long time and this too, will face restructuring. This numerical system is slowly easing into a twelve-based number system as we break through the next barriers of awareness. The base—twelve system is more compatible with the dimensional structures of creation we are moving into. It is of concern that we begin the re-education programs as soon as possible, with this potential expansion in mind.

Ingrained, man-made societal expectations such as the perception of separation between males and females are being subjected to changing thought patterns of the Mass Consciousness. When the great shift was initiated, the walls of the mine shaft in the Mini-miner analogy began to crumble and implode upon itself, releasing the old structures of their reality. In the same manner, the three-dimensional empires of the World are following the same pattern of cleansing. No new structures can be built until the old layers have been purified and recalibrated into a higher vibrational frequency. A car that is assembled with the highest level of technology is the one that can achieve, not only higher speed, but has the ability to tap into more sophisticated functions. Another analogy would be the act of renovating and rebuilding a house. Nothing can be rebuilt until the old structures have been dismantled.

We are travelling towards a new destination and are entering onto the stage of a new game. The fifth-dimensional game board is under construction and as a Mass Unit we decide on the arrangement of the new guiding rules, every step of the way. The ownership and responsibility of the playing field has been relinquished to our combined governing body. We are the new-born babes who are taking our shaky baby-steps and are learning the attributes of our new reality. We are at the cusp of a giant quantum leap into an existence in the higher hierarchy of existence. We are entering the Age of faster and higher Communication abilities that is the precursor into Interdimensional Communication Channels.

To increase the flow of light energies, each journeyman is encouraged to continually focus on heightened positive sensations, feelings, images of creative imaginations and thought patterns through the power of the words of light. The flow of the words that accumulated within the crystal cocoon and pulsed through the star tetrahedron form the energetic catalyst to boost the quantum leap in Consciousness. The words of light serve as a catalyst to open the channel of communication with the Divine Galaxy and the realm of Unity Consciousness, resulting in increased quantum sight for those on the path.

The petal of Mastery presents another insight in the mental-emotional body of the lightworker. It is the illusion of the coveted rank of the label of becoming a Spiritual *Master*. It tends to present a glamorous position on a platter of prestige. There are no labels, no titles of rank definitions, and no separations within the realities of Unity Consciousness in the higher realms. There are no pedestals, nor thrones erected within the world of Divine Love. The following contemplations are the thoughts of a number of individuals in respond to the question: "Who is a Master and what does Mastery stand for?"

A Master is perceived as one who has stepped out of the restrictive box of the challenges of the game of drama, by fully understanding how to be an enlightened human. He or she is a human who recognizes the opposing forces of Duality within the energies of Separation and has chosen to embrace the Oneness of All. These Masters accept the uniqueness of each member of humanity and every living entity they encounter. They have discovered the door that leads to the awakening of the Divine Self by releasing the human imprints accumulated through various lifetimes, thus freeing the Self from karmic shackles. There are no bars, walls or boundaries for the Master who has his or her internal sight on Divine Light and who continues to walk the enlightened path without any doubts or hesitations.

Earth Masters have gained the abilities to transform the heavy, dark emotional strands into crystalized love filaments of light. They embrace every experience as part of the human adventure and commit themselves to the process of Consciousness expansion of the Self. A Master is fully aware of the role of the Ego-self and has mindfully transformed the

Ego particles within all the layers of the body into lighter particles of supporting energies. Masters have released the need for any recognition and status, for they walk in complete awareness of *who they are*. Masters have no expectations of outcome and have stepped into a dedication of service to the Self and to all others. They voluntarily take on the job of anchoring the new human frequencies in the field of Divine Wisdom.

Mastery requires complete immersion and acceptance of the energies of Divine Love. The platform of Mastery only recognizes all facets of Unconditional Divine Love. No speck of dust or dirt chunks of any kind can attach itself to a radiating beam of light. In the same manner, no dark emotional particles can attach itself to pulsing, filaments of Love-Light.

All the Ascended Masters work together in the realms of Oneness of Consciousness, and the Goddess has asked that the message sent from Archangel Michael be gifted here. Spiritual Ego does not, and cannot exist in the world of Light and neither does the concept of ownership of any knowledge. Within the community of Oneness, the river of knowledge is open and free for anyone who is able to navigate its vast, flowing currents. Anything caught within it is freely shared and its wisdom gladly sown onto fertile minds.

Through the medium, Ronna Herman, Archangel Michael has provided his view on the subject of Mastery. It is a privilege for all human Masters to receive this gift of clarity and validation.

"A Master seeks the highest truth and lives it to the best of his/her ability.

A Master learns to view the world and its great drama from a higher vantage point. Time becomes malleable as you move out of the linear time-line into the spiralling, undulating vibrational waves of the higher dimensions.

A Master is adept at manipulating energy, always for the greatest good and exists in a vortex of harmonious spiritual forces.

A Master accepts that ascension is a mind and soul expanding process forever passing from one state of heightened consciousness to another.

A Master attains the first steps to self-mastery by entering into an age of conscious awareness and wakening to the nudgings of Soul-self.

A Master knows when to speak and when to be SILENT and is deliberate in his/her speech. He/she knows that constant mind chatter and senseless gossip disturbs the auric field.

A Master looks for the harmonious, higher waves of frequencies of Light in All things and strives towards increasing his/her capacity for Creator Light in constant effort.

A Master sees that knowledge alone divides while wisdom and Soul awareness unites.

A Master understands that when you deny any facet of your Divinity, you are denying your divine wholeness.

A master accepts and absorbs the following concepts of higher learning:

That the Universe is constantly remaking and redefining itself via the impulses and desires of the Supreme Mother-Father-God-Creator.

That the Supreme Creator's desire is to experience individuality by refracting itself into unimaginable number of various-sized sparks of consciousness, US.

That the Omniverse is filled with dancing, flowing, merging and separating fragments of God-Creator particles, us the God-Sparks.

That the Creator is alive and conscious in each and every one of these fragments, no matter how large or how small and no matter what color or what choices each spark makes.

That space is an entity within itself, waiting to be programmed or molded into infinite possibilities."

The depth of the Archangel's transmission was a profound message for humanity at large. The Master in human form acknowledges the roles it has to play. It wears the multiple mantles of the teacher, the guide, the healer, the facilitator, the scholar and at the same time wears the hats of the student, the apprentice and the humble servant in unconditional service.

It is the destination of the Master to strive towards equal partnership with the Angelic-Soul team and to reach the ultimate song of heavenly harmony. When each instrument has been attuned to the right resonating range, the orchestra is then ready to follow the Maestro's baton and burst forth into a glorious, harmonious performance. Human biology is a bioelectrical system and is considered to have attained complete health when its sound frequency is in perfect harmony with the vibration of the song of the Universal Life force. The auric field, as part of this electro-magnetic structure, emits waves of color frequencies that respond to specific sound vibrations. In a deep meditative state, it is possible to create a vortex of sound that leads us into a *STILL POINT* within the awareness of the High Mind. This is a space between the flow of thoughts, which is a moment in time where everything seems to stop, giving us the opportunity to retune and balance our inner music. It is one of the reasons that listening to resonating musical scores during meditation helps us to reach the point of stillness. Inner tuning happens when we begin to accept the *NOW* moment and to surrender to *WHAT IS* rather than insisting on holding onto *WHAT IS NOT*. Every atom, every molecule and in fact, our entire nervous system vibrates to various sound frequencies. Every organ is an instrument waiting to be recalibrated and tuned into the frequency of the high vibration of the Soul-Heart song. This master command performance of Unity Harmony is a joyful celebration that has been a long awaited occasion by the citizens of the Divine Omniverse.

In conclusion, it is worth repeating that fear-based emotion and the mental layers of the Ego-control issues either slow down the momentum, or put a complete stop to the spiritual journey. The expedition could be jeopardized into a life-long halt, with the human vessel stuck in park until further notice from its Soul-Consciousness. It stops the flow, the drive and the forward progression of the voyage and it is put on hold until the next incarnation. The astral waterways of the mental-emotional bodies become stagnant when thought patterns and heavy emotional reactions do not acknowledge and support the spiritual destiny before us. When we accept and embrace the changes, it dismantles the road blocks in every part of our being and a clear path to enlightenment and ascension appears in our guiding map. The cleared map will become our guide at the next incarnation thus guaranteeing a faster and easier travel on the path of enlightenment. Enlightenment is not an unobtainable distant destination, but the choice of living an expanded life filled with words of light, such as kindness, detached compassion and Unconditional Love. It is a conscious choice to walk away from fear because FEAR is but the absence of knowledge and Love. In the same vein, darkness is but the absence of Light for light is the manifestation of Love.

A great Soul, known among us as Nelson Mandela voiced his wisdom in his famous speech;

> *"Our greatest fear is not that we are inadequate. Our deepest fear is that we are powerful beyond measure. It is our light, not our darkness that most frightens us. We ask ourselves, who am I to be brilliant, gorgeous, talented, and fabulous? Actually, who are you not to be? You are a child of God. Your playing small does not serve*

the world. There is nothing enlightened about shrinking so that other people won't feel insecure around you. We are all meant to shine, as children do. We were born to make manifest the glory of God that is within us. It is not just in some of us; it is in everyone. And as we let our own light shine, we unconsciously give other people permission to do the same. As we are liberated from our own fear, our presence automatically liberates others."

The Divine Feminine Goddess within us yearns and seeks to love and to nourish us that we may blossom into balanced harmony. She brings us the energies of Divine Grace that assists us to manifest our potentiality of possibilities. She encourages us to surrender to our true nature and to fall in love with our own Divinity, our Divine-Soul partner.

Having presented us with the numerous informational guidelines, the Goddess Quan Yin presents us with the thought provoking questions, ***"Are you ready? Are you ready to grow into spiritual adulthood and step into the role of a guiding light along the Path of the evolution of Consciousness?"***

REFERENCES

Archangel Michael's free channeled messages are posted on Ronna Herman's site. *www.Ronnastar.com*. Contact *ronnastar@earthlink.net*

Lee Carrol channels the Kryon messages at *www.kryon.com*

Tyberon the Earth Keeper channels the messages from Metratron at *www.earthkeeper.com*

The Healing Power of Water, by Dr. Masaru Emoto

ABOUT THE AUTHOR

Shih Yin is an ordained Spiritual Minister in the area of metaphysics and spiritual energy healing. She began to channel the messages of the Goddess Quan Yin in 1995 and was given the name Shih Yin by the Goddess. Shih Yin has studied under many spiritual Masters and has dedicated her life to the Goddess Path which is the map given to her by Quan Yin. Based on the teachings of the Goddess, Shih Yin founded an Energy Healing modality to assist anyone who enters this Pathway. She has published three books previously under her registered name of Jinna van Vliet. The books are available as the Lotus Trilogy.

Made in the USA
Lexington, KY
27 February 2015